RE-CREATING A LIFE:

LEARNING HOW TO TELL

OUR MOST LIFE-GIVING STORY

RE-CREATING A LIFE:

LEARNING HOW TO TELL

OUR MOST LIFE-GIVING STORY

Diane M. Millis, PhD

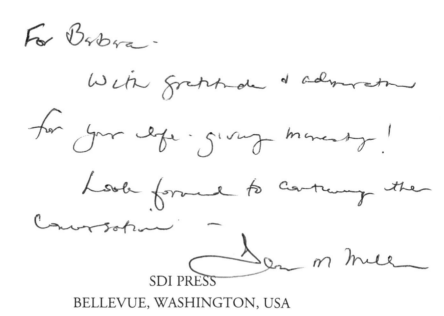

For Barbra -

With gratitude & admiration

for your life-giving ministry!

Look forward to continuing the

conversation -

Diane M. Mills

SDI PRESS

BELLEVUE, WASHINGTON, USA

SDI ● PRESS

Published by SDI Press, a division of Spiritual Directors International, 2025 112th Ave NE, Suite#200, Bellevue, WA 98004 USA.

www.sdiworld.org

ISBN: 978-1-950309-00-9

Cover design: Matthew Whitney

For Ryan

The telling is as much a redemptive act as are the acts that are told, for telling the story sets an example and provides an impetus for change.

—Dan McAdams, The Redemptive Self

Table of Contents

Foreword

Who are we, really?

Few questions are as essential as that one. Our identities hinge on the answers we provide, on so many levels, both mundane and transcendent. And our responses can change from moment to moment, especially transformative ones, when taking stock of ourselves is demanded.

In this extraordinary book, Diane Millis shares the power of narrative storytelling in shaping how we perceive ourselves, and how we are perceived by others.

A noted author and good friend of mine once told me that we shouldn't be worried about writing our autobiographies, as people don't read them for us, they read themselves into our stories.

Diane uses this approach with detail and elegance, hanging various storytelling techniques and tools around her own life. Basically, showing us how it can be done.

As we are guided through our shifting memories, fears, heroes, villains, uplifting moments, and heartbreaks, we start to get a true handle on the power of our own narratives. And as we do so, we begin to understand ourselves better, allowing us to reimagine who we are, and who we could become.

In the process, we come to terms with many of the characters in our life stories, in a particularly effective form of therapy.

Anyone and everyone can benefit from reading this book. With that said, and because spiritual companions are trained to carefully listen to the stories of others, they are particularly well positioned to understand the redemptive potential of shifting narratives.

It has been said that the universe is not made of atoms, but of stories.

In this book, Diane Millis illustrates how true that is, and how impactful our narratives are. Most importantly, she shows us how to get a handle on our stories so that they become tools at our disposal, rather than albatrosses around our necks.

Spiritual Directors International is proud to offer up this book as the launch of its new imprint, SDI Press, which will be devoted to exploring themes of concern to our community of spiritual companions.

Reverend Seifu Anil Singh-Molares
Executive Director, Spiritual Directors International

Prologue

There is a grace beyond all our plans.

— Jalaluddin Rumi

She had a goal for the summer she was turning 10: to be perfect for an entire day. For just one day, she aspired to behave perfectly, look perfect, *and most importantly—keep things in perfect order.*

Her quest began each evening before she went to sleep. She carefully arranged the items on her desk, dresser, and end table so that she could rest assured knowing that from the moment she opened her eyes, things would be in order. She figured that the perfect looking women who appeared on the covers of the magazines she had just started to read began their days in this way. Surely Chris Evert had a perfectly organized room.

She began each day with such great hopes. She would

— open her eyes, remember the quest;
— step out of bed, execute the quest;

However, when she

— opened the door of her bedroom,
    the quest was defeated.

Whether she ventured toward the bathroom or descended to the kitchen, something always conquered her. It could have been her sisters or her mother. Yet, most often, it was her own thoughts. The

3

reality was that *Operation Perfection* never lasted for even an hour, much less an entire day. Once she left her canopy bed, opened the door, and stepped out of her room, all bets were off.

She often preferred to just stay in her room, both literally and figuratively, rather than enter the hallway. Her room was the only place where she could exert some semblance of control. Except that is, for the days their cleaning woman dusted her room and carelessly set her treasures out of place. Aside from that, her room was the only place where she could linger without concern for her appearance. Her room was her sanctuary. It was there she could create, and follow, her own cadence. Once she left her room, she would be expected to smile.

She didn't always feel like smiling.

***

Looking back at my younger self some forty years later, it seems such an odd endeavor. Of all the things I might have aspired to be or do, why a quest for perfection? What about Micah's quest to *act justly, love tenderly, and walk humbly with God?* The perfection I sought was unrelated to any virtues such as *be ye perfect as your father in heaven is perfect* (which I later learned had nothing to do with achieving flawlessness but rather the aspiration to be perfect in love). No, it was the appearance of perfection that drove me—*that drove us*. My family was concerned with maintaining the illusion of perfection one finds displayed on magazine covers, in showcase homes, and at cocktail parties.

In August of the summer of 1972, I turned 10. Later that month, my parents informed me, and my younger sisters, that they would be separating. They told us they would try to work things out, and they did in fact try. However, three is a crowd. It turned out my father had been involved for many years with another woman. No matter how perfect my behavior might have been for a day or even a portion thereof, I would soon discover that putting things into perfect order was beyond my control.

The following school year I missed countless days of school, first with pneumonia, then with migraine headaches. In early May, before the school year had even ended, my mother packed up a car and moved my sisters and me from our home in Minnesota to Phoenix, Arizona. Almost as quickly, my dad remarried. By the summer of '73, my life was so far from perfection, I scarcely recognized it.

The new project, if I had thought to name it, might have been called *Project Endurance*. I did my best to endure living in the Valley of the Sun, yet it felt far more like a valley and I have little recollection of the sun. I missed my father, I missed my friends, I missed my extended family, and I missed my beloved Catholic school. I missed *being somebody* even if I wasn't a perfect somebody.

★★★

Those who have lost limbs report feeling excruciating pain even though their body part is no longer present. It's called a phantom limb. Ever since my parent's divorce, I've lived with a phantom life. Without consciously realizing it at first, I continually compared the life that I was living to the life *I might have lived* by telling myself two stories:

1) There was the story of the girl whose life might have been perfect had it not been for her parents' divorce and all the repercussions that event had on her life. And, . . .

5

2) There was the story of the girl who wasn't perfect, who was often depressed and disengaged, who no longer felt at home in her own home or her own skin. When asked how she liked living in Phoenix, she'd retort: "As soon as I'm 18, I'm moving back to Minnesota." She assumed that would still give her time to *get her life back.*

And sure enough, I did move back to Minnesota for college, and have lived here ever since. Yet in spite of this, this story about *the life I might have lived* did not disappear. It persisted.

At 55 I still, on occasion, hear its subtle refrain. I continue to wonder how much better my life might have been had I not experienced the disruptions of my parents' divorce and our subsequent relocation.

My presumed answer: much better.

As a participant in a recent retreat I facilitated observed, "I can't rewrite history." And she is absolutely correct. We cannot rewrite history. We cannot go back and change the details of our lives regarding what occurred, when, and with whom. Yet, **we can re-author** the stories we tell about our history.

As narrative therapist Alice Morgan underscores, "Our lives are multistoried. There are many stories occurring at the same time and different stories can be told about the same events. No single story can be free of ambiguity or contradiction and no single story can encapsulate or handle all the contingencies of life."[i]

As much as I might have wished otherwise, I can't edit out my parents' divorce, can't edit out having to relocate to another part of the country, can't edit out the depression I suffered from, can't edit out the poor choices I made in my youth.

Yet I can learn to tell a different story about those events. Through reflection, writing, and conversation with others, I can re-examine the meaning these events have for me today and listen for a new story waiting to be told. I can re-create my life through the story I tell about it, and so can you.

Is your life what you thought it was going to be? Perhaps you too have a phantom life, that is—you compare the story of the life you wished you had lived with the life you are actually living.

One of the primary reasons that people seek the accompaniment of a spiritual director, therapist, or other listening professional is to try to make sense of the disparity between what they thought their lives were going to be and what they actually are. They seek assistance in making meaning of their lives.

Whether or not our lives are what we thought they were going to be, Rumi reminds us, "there is a grace beyond all our plans."

Our stories are never complete or finished. There is always more meaning, more revelation, and more grace waiting to be found.

There is always another story waiting to be told.

***

Introduction

Within the multiplicity of stories that inform our lives and acts of living, some narratives take over and start to dominate. This dominant problem-saturated story then closes down the richness of identity and living, resulting in thin conclusions about one's identity. And yet, the alternative narrative is always present, patiently waiting to be seen, to be invited back more fully into the preferred way of living and being.

—Chené Swart,
Re-Authoring the World

After her mother started working full time, Chené's father took her aside. Although she was only ten, he said that she would now need to become the other woman in the house. It was on that day, Chené Swart observes, that the story of *Silent Servant* was born. *Silent Servant* is the name Swart gave to the story that dominated her identity and behaviors for the next three decades of her life.[ii] It was a narrative that she rarely questioned or resisted.

Swart recounts how the world she inhabited as *Silent Servant* was supported by taken-for-granted ideas and beliefs held by her Afrikaner Christian culture. The sociocultural scripts of the patriarchal culture in which she was raised included:

- good daughters should honor their parents;
- good women should care for men and children;

- all women should remain silent and not express discontent; and
- women's selfless care for others is more important than their care of self.

And so Swart, the *Silent Servant*, persisted in giving her life away for her family, her religious community, and her God even though her body eventually started to rebel. (She reports suffering from glandular fever, an underactive thyroid, and high cholesterol.)

Until one day she did the unthinkable: she spoke up at a meeting in her religious community and challenged things that were being said. As a result, she was rebuked, isolated from the community, and told she needed urgent psychological help.

The Stories that Drive Us, The Stories that Draw Us

Each of us is born into a particular constellation of narratives, an assortment of taken-for-granted ideas and beliefs. These stories that we receive from our family, faith tradition(s), culture, and society become the lens through which we view reality. For the first decade or more of our lives, we are largely unconscious of the stories that hold us; we are also unaware of their impact on both our identity and our agency.

It's as if each of us enters life as a passenger sandwiched in the middle of the back seat of a car. We have no control as to where the car is being driven, our view of our surroundings is partial at best, and we are utterly dependent upon our fellow passengers to provide details about the sights along the way. We have no realization that there are other cars in which to drive, other destinations to which to travel, other passengers with whom to travel, and even other means of transportation! All we know is the car we've been in; all we know are the narratives we've been told. We move through life *driven* by these stories, unconscious of them, and unaware of the tremendous power they hold over our thoughts, feelings, and actions. Whether the stories we are told prove helpful or harmful to our eventual outlook, they are ours and we are invested in them.

Optimally, at some point in late adolescence or young adulthood, we get out of the back seat of the car we've been in, take stock of where we've been, with whom we've traveled, and the stories we've heard along the way. We consider what stories we want to hold on to, what stories we want to resist or release, and with whom we want to travel as we journey onward.[iii]

We do not need to remain dependent upon nor limited by the stories that have been driven into us.

Each of us has the capacity to author a new story: a story that we prefer, a story to which we are drawn.

Yet, how do we begin to author a new story for our lives?

Re-Creating Our Story

Because stories and identities are negotiated within communities, the re-writing and re-authoring of alternative stories can never be a solo endeavor.

—Chené Swart,
Re-Authoring the World

11

It takes a community to help us learn how to tell a more life-giving story. We do not become a self on our own, nor do we author our story in isolation. Audiences are vital to the creation of our self and our story. Persons of all ages need listeners who are willing to mine the meaning in their stories with them: that is, one or more persons who will encourage us to dig deeper and consider alternative interpretations of the stories we tell.

So let's return to Chené Swart's story. Swart assembled a community of concern consisting of friends and colleagues she met in graduate school. [iv] With them, she began to explore the exceptions to her story of *Silent Servant*. They encouraged her to examine unseen storylines, that is, those times in her life when she didn't remain silent but instead spoke and led boldly. They also helped her to enhance her understanding of what she had learned from *Silent Servant's* contribution in her life:

- She taught me how to work hard and relentlessly, sometimes without pause or rest;
- She always kept her word;
- She entered into and opened up relationships in service of others;
- She took away the fear of adults;
- She laid the foundation for my character;
- She taught me to pay attention to other people's needs; and,
- She taught me how to really listen. [v]

Through the synergy of storytelling in community coupled with a commitment to personal introspection, Swart re-authored her story. She now names her story: *The Voice of Transformation in This World.* [vi]

Who we are and what we do are influenced by the stories that we tell about ourselves. While we can't always change the stories that others have about us, we can influence the stories we tell about ourselves and those we care about. And we can, with care, rework or rewrite storylines of identity.

—David Denborough,
Retelling the Stories of Our Lives

How aware are you of the story you are telling yourself? Becoming mindful of our inner narrative is crucial, because the story we tell ourselves, both consciously and unconsciously, has tremendous power over our thoughts, feelings, and actions.

Are you enacting a storyline that has been authored and imposed upon you by others?

Are you living out of an incomplete, untruthful, or limiting narrative?

I know I have been, as you will read in the following pages.

Our stories are like prisms. In order to see the fullness of a prism, we need to hold it up in the light, turn it over, and examine it from every direction. Optimally, when we tell our stories, we do the same. We hold our narratives up to the light; we turn them over, and examine them from every direction. Yet each of us can view only one side or dimension of a prism at a time, that is—the side that is most visible to us. We need other people who can help us to see the light in our story refracted from their vantage point. We benefit from the accompaniment of committed listeners who help us to see both aspects of our story *and ourselves* we may otherwise miss.

13

Let me offer an example to illustrate. Remember the story I told in the prologue about the little girl who aspired to be perfect for just one day?

It wasn't until I was in my mid-30's that I remembered this story for the first time. I wrote it out yet had no intention of ever publishing it. Yet, it wasn't until I was in my mid-50's that I told it to anyone for the first time. I can still see in my mind's eye the booth where we were seated the afternoon I read the story to my colleague Busshō. No sooner did I finish than he exclaimed, "*Oh I just love this little girl. All she wants is to be perfect for just <u>one</u> day. That's it, just one day. And I feel such compassion for her because she doesn't even make it for just one hour. Yet, she doesn't give up, she keeps trying and aspires to try again the following day.*"

I was shocked by his response. I said to him: "*Love this little girl?* How can you *love* this little girl? She's so obnoxious. I mean of all the things that could have preoccupied her for a day or more, she chooses to be perfect? That seems pretty self-absorbed to me."

(And he replied, "but she's so genuine in her aspiration.) I wonder what it was that stoked her quest for perfection."

His question cut right to my core. Indeed, there was *a lot* that was stoking her quest for perfection that I honestly hadn't considered as I wrote out the story. And Busshō helped me to see *the unseen storylines* in this little girl's life at the time. She wasn't entirely self-absorbed; she was trying to save her family. She must have thought that by behaving perfectly, she could create order in the midst of the emotional chaos.

As we continued to talk about her story, *I began to see her through his eyes*, and I too started to feel a sense of compassion for her.

Exploring Our Stories: Noticing, Appreciating, and Wondering

The manner in which Busshō responded to my story is the approach I often teach students and workshop participants. I invite them to pay attention to what they notice, appreciate, and wonder about as they listen to one another's stories. In my case, he . . .

noticed and named his affection and admiration for the story's protagonist;

appreciated her intentionality, her genuineness, her tenacity;

wondered about what would motivate such a young girl to embark on such a quest.

Like Busshō, we can learn to pay attention to what we notice both in the other's story and *in ourselves* as we listen, to name what we appreciate in the story, and to offer what we wonder about and want to explore further with the storyteller. Unlike Busshō, we need not be long-term friends in order to do so.

I now tell the story about my ten-year-old self in an entirely different way. Although the details remain the same, the interpretation I hold is fresh and new. Seeing her through his eyes helped me cultivate greater self-compassion. My friend helped me discover how to tell a more-life giving story.

An Invitation

You are the story you tell yourself, so tell yourself a good story.

15

—Francois Kiemde,
an interview participant for *Lives Explored*[vii]

All of us need to learn how to tell a good story. This book is designed to help you develop your capacity to discern how to tell your most life-giving story.

For over three decades, psychologist Dan McAdams has studied the stories people tell about their lives. He has found that the most generative adults tell more redemptive stories. What is a redemptive story? A redemptive story features a negative life event. It then describes how the event was redeemed by positive outcomes or narrates how the storyteller found positive meanings in the negative life experience. Those with a redemptive outlook believe that suffering is inevitable, yet they keep their hope alive through the stories they tell themselves, and through the stories they tell others.[viii]

For almost three decades, I have had the privilege of serving as a midwife for others as they give voice to the vast array of stories inside of them. Through teaching and advising undergraduate and graduate students, consulting and coaching in a wide array of sectors, facilitating retreats and leading workshops, producing a video narrative series and ministering as a spiritual director, I have observed, listened, and inquired as participants discern how to tell their most life-giving stories—stories to which they are drawn.

This book invites you to do the same. It is designed as a handbook for your narrative explorations and structured around guiding questions that encourage you to:

- Discover the story you are currently telling yourself;

- Develop your capacity to re-create your story through the telling of alternative stories;
- Discern the story that is waiting to be told by you and through your life.

The guiding questions in the following pages have all been road tested. I have posed them in the courses I have taught, the retreats and workshops I have led, and the conversations I have shared with spiritual directees. While the list is not exhaustive, it is designed to be evocative for both those who are just beginning to author their story as well as for those who continue to re-author theirs. My hope is that the questions featured in the following pages prove to be accessible to people of various ages, cultural, and religious backgrounds. One doesn't need to know how to read or even write in order to participate in this quest of authoring a life story, as we are storytellers by nature. For thousands of years, we have transmitted our wisdom through the stories we are told and then tell.

This book is framed around four guiding principles:

1. **Any story can provide a portal.** We don't need to start at the beginning of our lives and recount our narratives chronologically. David Drake observes in his book *Narrative Coaching*: "In my experience, it does not matter which stories people choose to share first. They will begin at the level at which they are ready, and the critical themes will be forthcoming regardless of where they begin. Any story or set of stories can be a portal into the larger issues at play and the path for people to reach their resolution or aspiration." [ix] While the questions in this book are listed in a chronological fashion, inviting you to look back at the story you tell yourself

about who you've been, then move to the story you are telling yourself about who you are now, before turning to the story you aspire to tell about your future self, give yourself permission to respond to them in your preferred order. You may opt to begin your narrative exploration with the question to which you feel the most drawn.

2. **Any other person's story can provide a portal into one's own.** Each of the following chapters invites us to tap into the stories we hold in response to a guiding question—a narrative prompt. I begin by telling my own stories in response to each prompt, and then invite you to tell yours. I offer my stories as a gateway, a catalyst, to invite you to enter more fully into your own. In his book *The Way of All the Earth*, John Dunne describes the adventure of *passing over* to other religious traditions and then *passing back* to one's own.[x] Walking in someone else's "religious moccasins" potentially increases our understanding of the fit in our own. My hope is that as you read my stories, you will *pass over* into my lived experience and then *pass back* with greater insight into your own.

3. **Any person can accompany you.** One need not be trained as a listening professional in order to serve as a deep listener. While I don't want to undermine how invaluable it can be to meet and examine your story with a listening professional, I also don't want to perpetuate the belief that it is only trained or licensed professionals who can help us discover more meaning in our stories. My own life experience has taught me again and again that this is not the case. My most exquisite experiences of being listened to deeply were the conversations

I have shared with teachers, caring adults, family members, and dear friends. I have learned more from the insights they helped me to see and hear than the hours I spent meeting with listening professionals in my youth and young adulthood.

4. **Any narrative can offer more revelation.** Over the course of my life, the story I have shared the most often and with the most audiences is the story of the impact my parent's divorce, and our subsequent relocation to another part of the country, had on me. At some point, one would think I would be finished telling that story. Yet, in writing this book, I continue to see new aspects of that ever-evolving narrative, and even more importantly a larger narrative arc in which that story resides. The more I work with my own narrative, and accompany others as they do the same, the more I awaken to the reality of co-creation and rely on the Spirit's co-authoring. We are all being held in a limitless narrative frame: our stories and Love's action in them are never complete or finished. The invitation to re-create our lives through the stories we tell about them is a life-long quest. May we all be given the "eyes to see, and ears to hear" our most life-giving story.

***

Who cares? What in the world could be less important than who I am and who my father and mother were, the mistakes I have made together with the occasional discoveries, … But I talk about my life anyway because if, on the one hand, hardly anything could be less important, on the other hand, hardly anything could be more important. My story is important not because it is mine, God knows, but because if I tell it . . . the chances are you will recognize that in many ways it is also yours. Maybe nothing is more important than that we keep track, you and I, of these stories of who we are and where we have come from and the people we have met along the way because it is precisely through these stories in all their particularity, . . . that God makes himself known to each of us most powerfully and personally. If this is true, it means that to lose track of our stories is to be profoundly impoverished not only humanly but spiritually.

—Frederick Buechner,

Telling Secrets

In an era of 24/7 news coverage, when we are bombarded with stories of every stripe, why should we care about devoting time to telling our stories to one another? What difference does it make to person on the other side of the world (or even the other side of my block) if I share the story of my childhood aspiration to be perfect for just one day?

Because telling our stories sets us free…

… from the walls that separate us and isolate us; in sharing our stories with one another we connect with the commonality of our shared human condition found at their root.

… from the hollowness and despair that can creep into our consciousness; in giving voice to our stories we remember the sacred Mystery at their source.

… from the limited viewpoints we often hold about our own and others' lives; in authoring our stories we become more fully who we were created to be.

***

Part One:
Discovering the Story You Are
Telling Yourself

What's your story?

The most important story we ever tell is the story of our lives.

—Dan McAdams,
The Art and Science of Personality Development

What's your story? Most of us, when asked this question, offer a stock, rehearsed reply. We often start with information about where we're from, our marital/family status, what we do for a living, and then add a distinguishing feature or two about our life journey such as *I was an army brat, so we moved a lot* or *my mother died was I was seven* or *I am a cancer survivor.*

In addition to the story that we tell others about ourselves, *we each have a story that we tell ourselves about ourselves.* We may not even be aware that we are telling ourselves a story. There are numerous adults with accomplished lives who are enacting a storyline that they are not even consciously aware of participating in—a story that has been authored and imposed upon them by others. They are stuck simply because they are unaware that they can write a different story from which to live and grow.

Take, for example, my dear friend Ted (a pseudonym). Ted's wise, he's witty, and he has a big heart. I really enjoy sharing time with him. Yet, each time I see Ted, he inevitably ends up telling me, "I haven't lived up to my potential." It's as if I walked up to a jukebox, put in a quarter, and pressed the song, "Not Lived Up to My Potential." The same story plays on.

25

Yet, I suspect that if you met my friend Ted, and learned more about his life, you wouldn't say: *now there's a guy who hasn't lived up to his potential.* Instead, you'd probably focus on the many ways in which he has devoted his life to serving others: through his career in teaching, through his marriage of over forty years, three children, and grandchildren, through his care for his aging mother, and through a second career as a home designer and builder.

So, it begs the question: what is fueling the story he is telling himself?

Is it that Ted had a lot of responsibilities in his family of origin, and almost all of his free time as a child had to be devoted to helping out with his family's business?

Is it that Ted's the second oldest child in his family? Ted's older brother is a physician; and Ted also attended medical school. Yet after a year, he decided it wasn't the best path for him. Does he feel he hasn't lived up to his potential because he didn't reach the potential he perceives his older brother did?

Is it that Ted got married at a young age, and between having kids coupled with working with even more kids in his career as a teacher, he no longer had the time (or energy) to pursue and cultivate his potential as an artisan?

Even though I've known Ted for years, I'm not entirely sure what has shaped the story he continues to tell. I'm also unsure if Ted is aware of the impact the story he is telling himself is having on him. I know the impact it has on me as I listen. I find it draining. And it leads me to wonder: given that he is now in his mid-60's, retired, and independently wealthy, does his internalized narrative (rather than current circumstances) keep him from *developing more of his potential?*

***

Each of our lives is an unfolding story. There is more than one way to tell our story. It's not what we've experienced that defines us, but the stories we tell about our experiences.

In *Composing a Life,* Mary Catherine Bateson highlighted the relationships, ever-evolving work, and pitfalls in the lives of five women. Bateson, an anthropologist, observed that none of these women's lives followed a single rising career trajectory from a set of pre-determined goals to a specific outcome. Rather, she documented the immense creative potential that can be wrought from the interruptions and conflicts we experience in our lives. She introduced a more fitting metaphor to characterize these women's lives— improvisatory art. She argued that instead of striving for constancy and continuity in an age where fluidity and discontinuity are central: "We need to look at multiple lives to test and shape our own."[xi]

I wholeheartedly agree, and would add: **we also need to look at our own life and test out multiple narratives.** This is the transformative potential that storytelling offers us. Our stories are not set in stone. They are malleable, and open to new interpretations throughout our lives.

Nonetheless, it is important to emphasize that **any story we tell is ultimately incomplete.** Our stories are guideposts, in that any story refers to something beyond the current narrative, or as the Zen tradition might say, "fingers pointing to the moon, not the moon itself." Therefore, our aim is to hold whatever story we are currently telling lightly not tightly as we investigate what further truths our story wants to tell us.

To tell a more life-giving story, we begin by increasing our awareness of the story we are currently telling ourselves.

What about you? Are you willing to give it a try?

Storytelling

- What is the story you typically tell in social situations?
- How aware are you of the story you are telling yourself about yourself?
- How does the story you are currently telling yourself about yourself make you feel?

What would you name the book about your life?

What story is worth your life?

—Lisa Marshall

One way of telling the story of my life is to start with the nursery rhyme Humpty Dumpty. Remember him?

Humpty Dumpty sat on a wall,

Humpty Dumpty had a great fall;

All the king's horses and all the king's men

Couldn't put Humpty together again.

I could relate to Humpty. Before my parent's divorce and our subsequent relocation to another part of the country, I was a little girl who was seated atop a seemingly sturdy wall. I felt like *a somebody* in every aspect of my life. My dad was a professional in our community, and my mother had a knack for making our lives look beautiful. I loved my school, did well as a student, and was viewed as a leader by many of my teachers/peers.

And then I had a great fall. My parents divorced, and my mother decided that she needed to relocate in order to begin anew. Living in the same town as my father, and his new wife, was not an option for her. So two weeks before the end of my fifth grade year, she packed us up—my two younger sisters and me—and we drove to the Valley of the Sun. While my mother did eventually rise like a phoenix from

29

her ashes, I remained in the dust. I refer to the years I lived in Phoenix as my desert years, both literally and figuratively.

So let's pause for a moment, and reflect on the story I've told so far. Psychologists would observe that this story (and Humpty Dumpty's) features **a contamination sequence**. That is, X happens (my parents divorce and we relocate) and after it does—one's life will never be as good as before X happened.

Just like Humpty Dumpty, after I fell off that wall—all the king's horses and all the king's men couldn't find a way to put either of us back together again. Throughout my middle, high school, and college years, I met with various counselors. And, when I did, I continued to tell myself the following contaminative story:

I had fallen. I had been broken by the divorce and even more so by having to leave my home, my school, and my family in Minnesota. If you had asked me then what I would have named the book of my life, I would have told you: *Broken Apart*. I didn't believe I could ever be put back together into some semblance of intactness, or if I could— it wouldn't happen until I returned home to Minnesota.

After seven years of living *in exile* in Arizona, I did return to my promised land of Minnesota. Nonetheless, I continued to feel like a damaged container. Throughout my college years, although I did my best *to appear intact*, I was aware that there was a crack in me. I resented that my life had been marred in this way.

The year I turned 24 was a watershed year. It was the year that I got married, started graduate school, and began meeting with a spiritual director. It was the combination of all three of these key factors—receiving the unconditional love of the man I married, studying and teaching about topics that gave me insight into my life, and meeting with a spiritual director who helped me to turn my focus from attaining perfection to practicing self-compassion—that were pivotal in my beginning to re-author and tell a more redemptive story.

Over the past thirty years, I am learning to see that it was *through* the heartbreak of my parent's divorce and the displacement I felt living in another part of the country that I found my vocation. I discovered a depth in myself through the unexpected suffering I experienced so early in life. While this realization didn't mitigate the sense of broken heartedness I had felt and still feel, I have slowly begun to tell a different story about *the fruits of the heartbreak.* Those devastating experiences increased my compassion, my willingness to be vulnerable, and my commitment to accompanying those who are experiencing heartbreak. As a result of this realization, I would now rename the book of my life, *Broken Open.*

Yes, indeed I have been broken. There is no disputing that history. Yet, as I continue to work with and discover new meaning in my story, I identify less with Humpty Dumpty and instead turn my attention to an image offered by a wise Sufi master, Hazrat Inayat Khan:

"God breaks the heart again and again and again until it stays open."

I now ask myself an entirely different question. Rather than, "How much better would your current life be if your parents hadn't divorced and you could have remained at home in Minnesota?" I now ask: *Who would I be today if I hadn't experienced those heartbreaks?*

I've always wondered how *she* would have turned out. And, truth be told, I'm not sure how much I would have liked her. Yes, she was a sensitive girl, a bright girl, a curious girl, and often a caring girl. Yet, I don't think her compassion quotient would be the same as mine. I suspect she would have continued to fall prey to the illusion that perfection was something she could have attained. I also suspect that she would have felt driven to focus her attention on the outer life, on surface matters, on appearances rather than tending her inner life.

Falling off that wall broke me open to the source of my life's deepest meaning: the sacred wellspring of wisdom within me— within each of us.

Storytelling

- What would you entitle the book about your life?
- How, if at all, has your book's title changed over the course of your life?
- How many chapters does the book about your life include? What would you name each of them?

What is the fairy tale version of your story?

Human beings are not powerless in the face of the tyranny of life stories. We have inherent agency to shape our stories by making choices about which stories we will highlight.

—HyoJu Lee,
Redeeming Singleness[xii]

Once upon a time . . .

there lived a little girl who was raised to be a princess. Her father, an aspiring king, claimed to adore her, yet rarely lingered long enough to look at her closely. He told her that some day she should go to college so that she could tell people at cocktail parties that she had graduated from the University of Minnesota. Her mother, enamored with tales of Camelot, did her best to satisfy the king yet her best wasn't good enough. The aspiring king left the queen and their three little princesses. He married a wanna-be queen well before his little girl completed college. Nonetheless, the little girl completed college. Along the way, she discovered how much she truly loved learning. So much so, that she no longer wanted to be a princess; she wanted to be a professor. Yet the more time she spent in the land of higher education, the more she noticed how many professors rarely look closely with the eyes of their hearts or listen deeply with the ear of their hearts. She knew that there must be a place where these ways of being reigned supreme. She traveled far and wide in search of such a place. After much travail, she concluded that in order to find the place, she would have to create it by tending her own heart, and by following only that to which her heart felt drawn. What she most wanted to learn, she began to teach: to look closely and see others in the manner she most desired to be seen; to listen deeply and hear others in the manner she most yearned to be heard; to linger intentionally with others rather than rushing off to the next person or place. She eventually traveled far and wide creating places, for and with others, to cultivate these ways of being. As she did, she experienced joy beyond measure. And let the record show that along the way, she declined numerous invitations to cocktail parties.

It's not a long tale, barely over 250 words. Yet this condensed story probably conveys more about who I am and what I have grown to love and value (as well as what I had to overcome in order to do so), than just about anything else I've ever written.

***

Inviting participants to write the fairy tale version of their life story is often the first narrative invitation I extend to workshop or retreat participants. It is an unintimidating, playful starting point to begin writing in a beloved genre familiar to most of us. There is no way to do it wrong. The only requirement is that one's tale begin with the words: Once upon a time . . . .

In the workshops I facilitate, participants are given fifteen minutes to write out their story. Most tales take up no more than a single page.

I read my own example to get them started, but do not analyze or unpack the tale I tell.

After fifteen minutes has elapsed, I invite participants to pair up. Each person has a turn to tell (or read) their tale to their partner, and

I then ask both the teller and the listener to reflect upon the following questions:

Teller: What, if anything, did you discover about your story through the telling?

Listener: What did you learn about the storyteller through the telling?

After they've discussed the first person's tale, the second person then shares his or her tale.

Time and again, I hear from listeners, even those who know one another well, how they discover something new about the other through hearing their fairy tale. And, without exception, the storytellers glean new insight into their own stories.

***

So what did I, Diane, discover about my story through telling it as a fairy tale?

I see the scripts or myths at work in my story, beginning with the sociocultural scripts for femininity that so dominated our American society in the early 1960's. I was born in 1962, at the apex of an administration whose president and first lady aspired to be associated with the mythology of Camelot. My parents, in their mid-twenties at the time, followed suit. It was all about maintaining appearances. Although they may have been struggling in their marriage, just as the Kennedys were, if things *appeared to be beautiful,* most folks assumed it was.

Moreover, this concern with appearances was a dominant message I received from my father and his family of origin. As a little girl and oldest grandchild, I intuited that the way I looked was valued more than what I thought; agreeableness superseded honesty; charm surpassed courage. While I was blessed with a pleasant appearance, I was also blessed with a deeply reflective spirit. I have often wondered whom I would be today if my inner life had been attended to as much as my outer life was.

However, the script in my mother's family was quite different. In many cases, being overly concerned with appearances signaled vanity, and my maternal grandfather always cautioned: *don't get the big head.* Although all four of my grandparents valued hard work and were people of deep faith, my maternal grandparents valued education for education's sake. I still vividly remember the joy that emanated from my grandfather's 90-year-old face as he recited poems he had learned in college. Indeed, his education was a precious gift that he treasured throughout his life. Moreover, my mother had evinced immense courage at a very young age. She had been raised on a farm, and it was there that she had contracted polio at the age of six. She worked hard to regain her capacity to walk, yet the weeks she spent in isolation took a toll on her in many ways. While one's health or husband may be taken from you, she continually emphasized that education was "something that no one could ever take away from you."

So as my fairy tale conveys, there were at least two dominant scripts at work in my family of origin: one we might call the princess's script, and one we might call the professor's. Both of these archetypal energies are a large part of me, and they will be for the remainder of my life.

Yet what I am learning from the responses of those with whom I have shared my fairy tale is that the princess part and the professor part of me need not be in competition with one another. Those who have listened to my fairy tale often ask me how I might reengage with the princess part of myself *on my own terms*. It's a grand question, as I have spent an inordinate amount of energy over the course of my life, and especially throughout my academic career, trying to <u>not</u> appear princess-like. For example, I dress conservatively and try to avoid princess-related activities (like polishing my fingernails).

Through the telling of this tale, I am beginning to reengage with the princess part of myself, to welcome her, to have compassion for that part of myself rather than ostracize or be ashamed of her. What the current version of my tale doesn't reveal is that I married a man who is in every way a prince and throughout our thirty plus years of marriage has treated me like a princess. Moreover, it was through our relationship and his consistent encouragement that I pursued the pathway to becoming a professor. And it was through our relationship that we gave birth to a prince of our own.

Learning to author, and continuing to re-author, our stories challenges us to uncover and expose the influential metanarratives or scripts that have proven limiting and liberating.

This version of my fairy tale helps me to name and claim what I have grown to value, and the vocation to which I have been called. Whether I'm a princess, a pauper, or a professor, I aspire to draw upon my heart as my most significant source of knowing: its beauty, wisdom, and love. These are the characteristics that I choose to highlight in my story, and the quote/unquote happy ending that all fairy tales aim to achieve.

Storytelling

- In a page or less, tell the story of the fairy tale version of your life.

  Once upon a time . . .

- After you've finished, take time to consider and share:

  What, if anything, did you discover about your story through the telling?

- Ask those who listened to your story to consider and share:

  What did you learn about the storyteller through the telling?

Part Two:
Developing Eyes to See and Ears to Hear New Stories

Who is the protagonist in your story?

One of the deepest longings of the human soul is to be seen.

— John O'Donohue

As I reread the story I have told so far, I must confess that this story is partial at best, and at its worst misses out on *some overlooked territories.*[xiii] There is an alternative story waiting to be told. You see, even if my parents had remained married, and even if I had remained visibly seated atop that wall in the comforts of that life, my story wouldn't necessarily have had a Hallmark ending. How can that be, you might ask?

Because she, the protagonist in my story, was not the happy camper you might presume her to have been as she sat atop that wall. Yes, she might have been visible and yes, she might have led a comfortable life. Yet, as her fairy tale conveys, she often felt overlooked and partially seen. What she most desired was to be seen. She wanted others to look beyond the externals of her social location and her appearance. She yearned for others to look at her closely and listen to her deeply.

One of the guiding principles of narrative practice is: the person is not the problem, the relationship is not the problem, **the problem is the problem**. In order to address the problem as the problem, narrative practitioners invite those with whom they work **to name the story that fuels the problem**. By inviting those who struggle with a problem to name the problematic story, which they place in capital letters, people can then explore the conditions that contribute to the

43

problem, as well as **the instances when the problem isn't present.** Those unique instances offer the basis for narrating an alternative, preferred story.[xiv]

In my case, I would name the story of the problem I was experiencing: *Partially Seen.* The sociocultural scripts for femininity that so dominated American society in the early 1960's asserted that a good girl, and a good woman, should do her utmost to look pretty, be poised, and act polite. The focus was on a woman's external behavior and appearance. I don't recall any recognition given to allowing women to express the inevitable ugliness, awkwardness, and anger that are part of the human condition. It was up to good girls to repress all of that stuff or in my case, as a Catholic good girl, to confess all that stuff. Given this reality, it's not surprising that *Partially Seen,* along with many other girls and women, suffered from depression in her teens and other periods in her adult life.

Partially Seen, a little girl with a rich inner life, learned to cope by spending a lot time in her room. It was there that she could imagine the life she would live as an adult, and the contribution she aspired to make in it through her teaching.

So, in this storytelling exercise, I have now named my protagonist and told her story in the third person.

Why the third person?

Telling our story in the third person develops our capacity to witness, rather than judge, ourselves. When we look at ourselves from the vantage point of ourselves as a character in our story, we cultivate a new way of *being in relationship with our self*—which tends to engender greater self-compassion.

The following questions to which I respond are the same questions you will be invited to respond to at the close of this chapter.

What is your protagonist's name and why was that name given?

Her name is *Wanting To Be Seen*. She was given that name because there is so much more to her than meets the eye. It is her inner life, that *which isn't readily apparent*, which she is most eager to share with others.

What does your protagonist find life-giving?

She loves to read, reflect, observe, ask questions, and engage in conversations— especially one-to-one. She relishes time in solitude so she can attend to what is going on within her. And, she greatly enjoys meeting with others and attuning to what is stirring in their hearts. She flourishes through connecting with her core in prayer and introspection, and connecting with others through looking and listening to them with the eyes and ear of her heart.

What does your protagonist find limiting?

She finds it excruciating to endure social situations where one must engage in small talk and social posturing. She prefers to stay in her room (or now as an adult—her home) rather than feign interest or waste her time in such exchanges. She doesn't want to spend any more of her precious time holding in, or feeling the need to hide, those parts of herself that may not be socially acceptable to express. Her biggest fear, as you will read about in the following stories (especially the story about one of the "villains" in her life), is that she will be overlooked.

What is your protagonist seeking?

She is seeking to spend as much time as possible around people and in environments where she can be real, or learn how to be real, and invite those with whom she gathers to do the same. She wants to be around those who possess curiosity and concern for the other, who are interested in that which lies deeper than the surface, and who look closely for the unique potentialities to be found in each person. She is seeking to teach more people how to connect to what is going on deep within them, as well as how to inquire about and listen for what is going on within the other.

Storytelling

In this storytelling exercise, I invite you to introduce us to the protagonist in your story. Observe yourself as if you a character in your life's story. Follow this character around in your imagination. You may find it helpful to tell the story of your protagonist in the third person.

- What is your protagonist's name and why was that name given?
- What does your protagonist find life-giving?
- What does your protagonist find limiting?
- What is your protagonist seeking?

What is one of your earliest memories?

I would never investigate a personality without asking for the earliest memory.

—Alfred Adler

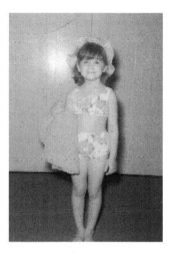

The lighting is awful, the quality of the photo poor, yet the memory is indelible. I was five at the time, and the girls in my dance class had been asked to serve as models for a fashion show.

I vaguely recall meeting at the dance studio the day of the big event: the hubbub of the other girls, their mothers circling about, the nervous anticipation and excitement in the air.

Yet, what I most remember is standing behind the curtain as I waited my turn. As I peeked between the slice where the curtains didn't fully meet, I could see all the lights that illuminated the runway.

I was ready. As soon as the girl before me opened the curtains, I stepped out in my first outfit: a two-piece swimsuit (pictured above) and I worked it. No longer five, I had the pep in my step of a twenty-five year old Miss America candidate in a swimsuit competition. I loved being in the spotlight. I smiled, I looked out at the audience, I walked with ease. While I don't know how many steps I actually took, I do know that I didn't make it to the end of the runway before the giggles and laughter woke me out of my trance. I felt confused. Laughter was not the response I had expected. Nonetheless, I pressed on to the end of the runway, turned, and made a beeline for the curtain. At that moment, what I most wanted to do was go home and read a book. Yet, that was not an option as I had been assigned one more outfit to model. I dutifully donned the navy blue sailor dress (is this why I never wear navy blue?). When my next turn came, and the curtains parted, I walked to the end of the runway, turned slowly, and made my way back to the curtain with as little expression as humanly possible. My objective was twofold: to finish, and to not arouse any more laughter.

***

There is much to be learned from our earliest memories. The psychologist Alfred Adler deemed his work with early memories to be one of his most important psychological discoveries. Adler believed *we have an active part* in what we remember. He found that through exploring our earliest recollections, we could glean insight into our personality—our tendencies, our biases, our purposes, and goals. What Adler found most telling was *how we responded to the situation* portrayed in our earliest memory rather than the situation itself.[xv]

48

So, how did I respond to the situation depicted in this story of my earliest memory? Looking back at this event through my eyes now, I recognize my resilience in response to what I perceived to be a humiliating situation. What I find noteworthy in this story is that I didn't run away and hide after modeling the first outfit. Rather, I upheld my commitment, and in so doing, adapted to the audience in the best way I knew how to at the time—by shutting down my expressiveness.

I now understand, after having been a parent myself, that the audience members weren't laughing *at me*, rather I suspect they found my precociousness to be endearing and engaging.

Yet I didn't know that at the time. How could I have? I was so embarrassed afterwards that I didn't discuss my feelings with my mother or anyone else. True to form, I kept it to myself. Yet had I done so, maybe others would have helped me to see a more truthful interpretation.

Yet in spite of this perceived humiliation, I didn't develop stage fright. Throughout my life, I have consistently enjoyed being on stage, teaching, and speaking. And yet, aligned with what happened that day, if I anticipate that what I am offering is not being appreciated in the manner I hope it will be, I shrink. I become subdued. I lose the metaphorical skip in my step. And, perhaps most importantly, I in turn hesitate to act as boldly as I would like to (as I fear being belittled for doing so).

Yet, forty-five years later, when I received a contract to write my first book, it was this picture of myself in that swimsuit which I placed right next to my computer screen. I needed to reclaim that little girl's chutzpah, her confidence, and her courage. I needed everything that that little girl brought to that moment *before* she stepped on to that runway.

What I most needed was *the skip in her step.* That's what strikes me most vividly. That skip captures her enthusiasm, her eagerness to step out into the world (or in this case on to the runway), and share herself fully. No holding back, no holding back.

Putting yourself out there is a huge risk, as that little girl learned. Yet, the older I get, the more I realize that if I shrink, play small, and go through the motions, there is even less of a chance that others will take the risk of sharing with me. It's up to me to model the way.

Storytelling

What's the story of your earliest memory? As you prepare to tell it, consider:

- What happened and who was involved?
- What thoughts and feelings did you remember having at the time?
- And, looking back at yourself then through your eyes now, what does *how you responded to the situation* tell you about yourself, your values, and your aspirations?

What fascinated and frightened you as a child?

Similar lists, dredged out of the lop side of your brain, might well help you discover you, even as I flopped around and finally found me.

—Ray Bradbury,
Zen in the Art of Writing

Ray Bradbury learned to develop his unique writing voice by making lists—lists of things that fascinated him, lists of things he feared. Here is one, among the many lists, that Bradbury generated over the course of his prolific writing career:

THE LAKE.

THE NIGHT.

THE CRICKETS.

THE RAVINE.

THE ATTIC.

THE BASEMENT.

THE TRAP-DOOR.

THE BABY.

THE CROWD.

THE NIGHT TRAIN.

THE FOG HORN.

THE SCYTHE.

THE CARNIVAL.

THE CAROUSEL.

THE DWARF.

THE MIRROR MAZE.

THE SKELETON.

If you are familiar with Bradbury's work, you can see how the nouns on this list found their way into his stories and the characters that inhabit them.

In his book, *Zen in the Art of Writing*, Bradbury talks about how he developed this method of gaining access to his subconscious. He describes how he would read over his lists, pick a noun, and then begin writing about it. Typically, by about mid-page, a story would emerge: "the stories began to burst, to explode from those memories, hidden in the nouns, lost in the lists."[xvi]

After reading about this method, I immediately wondered if generating such lists could give us insight into our own personal narratives, and how these lists of nouns might connect us to important stories we have long forgotten.

For me, I was fascinated by ...

The prie-dieu kneeler

The tunnel

The aquarium

The tabernacle

The metal chalkholder

And I was frightened by....

The river

The bridge

The catfish

The feeding tube

The basement drain

The prie-dieu

Entering my maternal grandmother's bedroom was like entering a temple. Often, in the midst of a family gathering, I would slip away to rest there. As I gazed at the twinkling candles atop her prie-dieu kneeler, I encountered a presence. This mysterious presence seemed to fill both the room and resound in the depths of my being—my heart. Over time, I noticed that this presence remained within my heart, regardless of whether or not I was in my grandmother's room.

My grandmother's room was one of the first places that helped me awaken to my heart—the life source within me. Although I knew that I couldn't control when this life source would burst open within me,

I was beginning to learn about the some of the conditions that prepared my heart for awakening to it: silence, solitude, stillness, and candlelight.

The catfish

If it had been up to me, I would have preferred to have only angelfish and guppies in my aquarium. Yet, it wasn't up to me. I was too young to care for my aquarium, and that yucky creature kept the tank clean.

Oh how I loved to watch those angelfish swim about. If I were a fish, I'd want to be an angelfish.

I so wished that catfish didn't have to mar the beauty of the tank with his presence. As hard as I tried to avoid looking at that fish, I was riveted to him.

What was a frightening object to me as a child, is now a source of fascination for me as an adult. I admire the catfish's great fidelity, how he swam about the tank's bottom ingesting the remains from my precious guppies and glorious angelfish. Moreover, the catfish offers me a powerful metaphor for my, for our, journey to integration: to cultivate awareness of both the angelfish and the catfish within us.

Storytelling

As you think back to your childhood,

- What were the objects in your environment that fascinated you?
- What were the things that frightened you?
- Generate your own list of nouns. Then choose one and see what story emerges.
- What objects that frightened you as a child now fascinate you as an adult?

Who is one of the heroes in your story?

Attention is the rarest and purest form of generosity.

—Simone Weil

Had I been offered the option of tele-transporting from fifth grade to adulthood, I would have immediately and emphatically responded: YES. I knew what I wanted to do with my life, and I knew who I wanted to become—Mrs. Hertzenberg, my fifth grade teacher. I'd be as pretty, poised, and polite as she, and I'd teach in a Catholic school (the older elementary grades, of course, as those younger grades are a bit too messy). Each day I, like her, would don a different hairstyle perfectly paired with my outfit. And, just like her, I too would be a paragon of equanimity and grace. I would never look tired; I would always appear rested and at ease.

In addition to navigating my parents' relationship, the other focal point of my fifth grade year was to replicate Mrs Hertzenberg's "look" (in an inconspicuous manner, of course). If she had worn a ponytail and a smock top with jeans, I would do so the next day. It kept me busy, as she never wore the same hairstyle for two consecutive days: they shifted from pigtails to a bun to a headband to barrettes. If she had discovered that I was imitating her, I would have been mortified. Yet, I wouldn't have had to worry; I knew that Mrs H. really liked me. She had given us, (that is me and my best friend Tracy), permission to rearrange the classroom desks in whatever way we wanted. And it probably doesn't come as a big surprise that I wished to have my desk front and center—in order to be as close as possible to Mrs. H's desk.

In spite of my fascination with this wonderful teacher, I missed a lot of school that year due to illness. My parents had separated a month before the school year began. I contracted pneumonia that fall, and suffered from migraine headaches that winter. I also missed the last couple of weeks of the school year, because my family relocated to Phoenix. After we had moved, my admiration for Mrs. Hertzenberg increased even more. I grew to see that she wasn't just pretty; she was beautiful. She had a tender, magnanimous spirit.

Authoring our stories invites us to reflect upon our intentions, influential relationships, turning-points, and treasured memories. [xvii] And for me, the story of Mrs Hertzenberg included all of them: my intention to become a teacher, the influential relationship I shared with her, the indelible impression she made on me at a key turning point in my life, along with the following treasured memory she helped to create for me.

The following school year, after I had finished sixth grade, I returned from Phoenix to visit my beloved Catholic school in Moorhead, Minnesota. It was the first visit I had made home since we had moved, and the only visit I would make there until I was well into adulthood.

Mrs. Hertzenberg was now teaching fourth instead of fifth grade. When she learned that I would be visiting, she asked if I would serve as her teacher's assistant for a day. Somehow she just knew that nothing would bring me greater joy, and she must have suspected that I had felt a bit nervous about returning, given how quickly my family had left and the reasons we had done so. Her invitation put me at ease. I now had an official role to play when I returned to my beloved school that day, along with plenty of time to spend reuniting with my friends in the sixth grade class.

When I am asked to tell a story about one of the happiest days of my childhood, it is this day that comes to mind. And it's no surprise to me that when I began writing my first book, it was these memories of Mrs. Hertzenberg, along with the recollections of so many other teachers who went the extra mile for me, that captivated my attention.

I was overwhelmed with the recognition of how influential teachers had been throughout my life, especially during its most challenging times. While some people have one special teacher who made an impact on them, I am blessed to have encountered many.

Today, Mrs. Hertzenberg would be in her 70's. I often wonder how long she taught for, where she now lives, and truth be told: what kind of hairstyle(s) she now wears. Two years ago, when I returned to my hometown grade school to offer a retreat, I tried to contact her. When I couldn't find anything about her online, I inquired at the school office to no avail.

If given the chance, I would want to thank her for her care and concern, to tell her the story I've written here about that memorable day, and to let her know that I too had become a teacher. While I still aspire to coordinate the look of my hairstyle with the outfit I am wearing as well as she did, what I most want to do is to emulate her beauty and tender heart.

Moreover, I would hope we would have enough time for her to share with me some of her own story. I so want to know: How did she learn to share her attention so generously? How did she develop such a tender heart? What did she find life-giving and limiting? What did she seek in her life, and what has she discovered along the way?

Storytelling

- Who is one of the heroes in your life story?
- What did this figure contribute to your life?

Who is one of the villains in your story?

I've learned that people will forget what you said, people will forget what you did, but people will never forget how you made them feel.

—Maya Angelou

All summer I had looked forward to being in her Advanced Health Class. I had had to apply, and felt fortunate to have been selected for one of the few spots available to juniors (thanks to my tenth-grade health teacher's recommendation). As I entered her classroom that afternoon, I saw them for the first time. Front and center, there they hung—the ten words that served as Ms. Errons' (a pseudonym) guiding principle—framed in a placard over her desk.

You never get a second chance at a first impression.

As a girl, I was accustomed to making good first impressions, or at least I had been.

Yet, from my very first day in Ms. Errons' class, I knew two things:

1) I would need a second chance at that first impression, and
2) I was never going to get it.

***

Smile and the world smiles with you.

Ms. Errons didn't seem to know about my mother's guiding principle. I had never seen Ms. Errons smile, nor even lift the side of

61

her lips. Would I dare to send a smile her way? Of course I did. Yet, it didn't seem to matter. I couldn't recall Ms Errons ever looking my way that entire spring semester, even though she had not only one but two entire class periods to do so each afternoon. It was the only class in our entire high school curriculum whose duration was two periods, and it just happened to be with the teacher who liked me least.

Why couldn't it have been Mr. Lassen's class that lasted two periods? I would have gladly endured two periods of Trigonometry just to be in his presence for two hours each day. In fact, I had intentionally demoted myself from the honor's section of trigonometry to the non-honor's section in order to continue to have him as my math teacher. One of the only highlights of my junior year was that I got to begin each day with Mr. Lassen's class. Surprisingly I often arrived a few minutes late, which may be totally acceptable for a social engagement, but highly unusual for a girl who considered herself late if she wasn't five minutes early. Yet, Mr. Lassen never reprimanded me for arriving late. He just smiled and said, *Thank you for joining us this morning.* He somehow seemed to know that care and vigilance was what I needed most, not reprimand and cross-examination. Perhaps he even noticed that as I exited his class, I turned right and walked on the perimeter of the high school campus rather than turning left toward its center to mingle among the masses. What I'm sure he didn't know is that my goal each morning was to try to make it through just one more day.

Ms. Errons informed us that each student was responsible for selecting a field trip site. Moreover, site selections were subject to her approval. Given our tenuous relationship, I played it safe. Rather than initiating an unprecedented visit to a new site, I stayed with Ms.

Errons' tried and true choices: we would visit the manufacturer of pigskin for victims in burn units located in downtown Phoenix.

The afternoon we embarked on the field trip to the pigskin plant, I got to ride shotgun with Ms. Errons. As the van made its way on I-10 from Tempe to downtown Phoenix, I seized my chance to change Ms. Errons' impression of me.

As Ms. Errons navigated her way through traffic, I navigated my way through some semblance of a conversation. Ms. Errons didn't make it easy. *If there are no second chances, there are no second chances.*

Yet, perhaps if …

Ms. Errons learned about the depression I'd been struggling with for the past six years since my parents' divorce, perhaps then she would make an exception and give me a second chance.

Perhaps if …

Ms. Errons knew that I was now meeting weekly with a counselor in an office in the administration building, she would surely loosen the grip of her first chance stance.

And if neither of those could move her, what if …

My friend Liz could tell Ms. Errons about the number of afternoons that I had spent with her witnessing her dying father reclining on the living room couch; how I had held her hand as she screamed at the sight of her father in his casket. Would any of that change Ms. Errons' impression of me?

Apparently not, as I later learned that Ms. Errons was the only teacher who had denied my nomination for the National Honor Society. Yet NHS paled in comparison to what really mattered to me most: I wanted Ms. Errons to *get* me. And I wanted to *get* Ms. Errons. I never understood what it was that I had done to tarnish her one and only impression of me.

If we could read the secret history of our enemies, we should find in each man's life sorrow and suffering enough to disarm all hostility.

—Henry Wadsworth Longfellow

I have no idea of Ms. Errons' story, what she had experienced, and what it was that led her to live by the maxim of no second impressions.

Ironically, Ms. Errons made an important contribution to my vocation. She served as a counter-example, the type of teacher I never wanted to be like. After my experience in her classroom, I vowed to be willing to look again. To try to give other people a second chance...and a third... to do my best to keep pushing the refresh button on the impressions I form, rather than allow them to ossify. I aspire to do so with my own students, and with more of the people I meet—even those who on first impression may appear to be villains.

Storytelling

- Who is one of the villains in your life story?
- What did this figure contribute to your life?

What experiences are you trying to see more clearly?

It is important to tell at least from time to time the secret of who we truly and fully are—even if we tell it only to ourselves—because otherwise we run the risk of losing track of who we truly and fully are and little by little come to accept instead the highly edited version which we put forth in hope that the world will find it more acceptable than the real thing.

—Frederick Buechner,
Telling Secrets

So many pivotal things occurred in my friend Libby's (a pseudonym) bedroom: it was there that I played the one and only game of Ouija I've ever played, it was there that I learned where babies really come from, and it was there that I remember reading that scary Reader's Digest story (was it Reader's Digest?) about a woman who had been abducted, buried alive, and was then fed by her abductor through a feeding tube. I remember being so terrified by that story, and so fixated on it, that I would practice timing myself to see how long I could lie unmoving in a confined space.

Yet, we didn't stay in Libby's bedroom on that particular night—the night of my first official sleepover. Instead, she and I slept on a double bed in the guest room on the main floor of her split-level home. I'm not sure why we slept there when we could have been upstairs in her bedroom each having a twin bed to ourselves. Nonetheless, at some point that night, Libby's older brother entered the guest room and made his way to the other side of the bed—the side on which I was sleeping. He woke me up, held up his hand to his mouth and gestured for me to keep quiet, before taking my by the arm and pulling me down the basement stairs to the laundry room. He pointed to the cement floor gesturing for me to lie down on it. He then lifted up my pink nightgown, pulled down his pants, and began moving his body part on top of my hips and stomach. I had no idea why on earth he was doing what he was doing, yet since I had been practicing lying really still, that is exactly what I did. A few minutes later, he put his body part back into his pants and pointed toward the door. I got up cautiously and then bolted back up the half set of stairs into the bedroom where Libby slept peacefully. I don't recall anything more about what happened afterwards. I'm not sure whether I got back to sleep or lay awake, whether I stayed for breakfast or left as soon as Libby woke up, whether I went over to her house again or stayed away. What I do know is that I didn't scream and I didn't tell a soul. A couple of weeks later one of my neighbors told me, in the midst of our two square game, about what had happened to her the night she slept over at Libby's. Yet even then I didn't say, *yeah that happened to me too.*

Almost a decade passed before I told anyone about what had happened to me that night. Since then, I have told my parents, my spiritual director, my husband, and our son. Yet it wasn't until very recently, almost fifty years after the incident, when I told two of my ministry colleagues about it. For the first time ever, I noticed the following question arise in me:

Why didn't I scream?

Well one answer is: I'm not a screamer. I was raised to be polite, to not raise my voice or yell, to strive to make myself heard in other more appropriate ways. Moreover, aside from the socialization script of behaving like a lady, I'm also pretty certain that as a guest in their home, I wouldn't have wanted to disturb anyone or inconvenience them—especially Libby's parents who slept two split levels above us.

And yet another answer is: I was terrified that had I screamed, he might have done something even more terrifying to me—that is, put me in a box, and buried me alive underneath the ground. I had to avoid angering him.

Yet, I can't help but wonder what would have actually happened if I had started screaming that night after Libby's brother tapped me on the shoulder.

What if I hadn't been as concerned about making sure others got a good night's sleep while I was being assaulted?

What if I had been as concerned about my own wellbeing as I was about Libby's, trying to protect her from the shamefulness of her brother's action?

I can hear my internal commentary: that was idiot compassion Diane. You were more concerned about being a good, obedient girl and ensuring others were comfortable than you were about yourself.

And then I also hear a more compassionate commentary: oh sweetie, you held so much in. You kept it to yourself. You weren't aware of other options; you were only six at the time and wanted to avoid an even worse outcome.

It's true. I did hold a lot in. It wasn't unusual for me to keep things to myself and try to not make a fuss. That very same year, when I was in first grade, as I slid to get up from the wooden lunch table, a sliver of wood lodged into my upper thigh. Rather than tell my teacher Sister Angela about it, I endured the remainder of the school day. I can still remember how close the desk in which I was seated was to the door, and how much I wanted to walk out and get help. Yet, I didn't want to cause a fuss. I knew that once I got home, my mother who was a nurse would take good care of me. Yet even she could not remove the wooden piece as it had lodged too deep. Later that afternoon, I remember hearing someone comment, as I lay face down on that clinic table after they had removed it: *how did she make it through the afternoon with this in her leg?*

Through my 50-something eyes, I see that six-year-old girl. And rather than fault her for her failure of courage, her refusal to scream, I see that she had, and still has, an immense capacity to hold tension. An inner resolve. She's not so much stoic as she is contained, and in turn, she can hold a container. It's proven to be an immensely important quality in my work as an educator, counselor, and facilitator. I typically don't freak out. I'm pretty good at maintaining non-anxious presence.

Yet, given how much I value life-long learning, I do see the next facet in her life's curriculum. It's about fierceness. Some things should not be contained. There are times when the only appropriate choice is to scream, to fight back rather than hold still. It is these new moves that I now aspire to practice.

Storytelling

- What experience are you trying to see more clearly?
- What thoughts and feelings does recalling this experience generate?
- And, looking back at yourself then through your eyes now, what do you currently see being revealed through this story?

What would you ask and tell your younger self?

If,
again
I have a chance to meet,
there is so much I want to ask
and so much I want to tell

—Chino Otsuka,
Imagine Finding Me[xviii]

It had been a whirlwind of a year. At the end of my junior year of high school, I decided to attend summer session in order to graduate a year early. Then, during my first year in college, I had been "discovered" by a renowned modeling agency and asked to move to New York City. I was now armed with my portfolio walking from one go-see to another, trudging up steps into dark hallways, and knocking on doors of photographers' studios filled with anxious young women. We all patiently waited our turn—that minute or two of partial attention that a photographer or client would offer as he (most often he) flipped through the photographs in our portfolios. They never looked at us deeply; instead their assessments were close to instantaneous. Either we had *it* or we didn't—the "look" that is.

Day after day that summer, I navigated my way to the next appointment. What I most recall is the sensation of the city's grime, coupled with the humidity, embedding itself into my skin. Unlike many folks I've met since then, I'd never been enamored with the thought of living in New York City. As a girl, I had seen the Macy's parades on television and watched the *Miracle on 34th Street*; yet my most vivid memories of the city stemmed from the television sitcoms *That Girl* and *Family Affair* that aired in the late 60's. What I liked most about those shows was not the city in which they were depicted; it was the relationships they shared there.

The life I most wanted to live was the one portrayed in the television show *Mary Tyler Moore*. I loved Mary, as did just about everyone with whom Mary came into contact. I wanted to live as Mary lived (except I wanted to be married), in the city where Mary lived (Minneapolis), and what I most wanted was to become as beloved as Mary was.

Yet here I was in New York City. Within a couple of weeks following my arrival, I started getting booked for work. Modeling paid well and my game plan was to bank the money I earned so I could resume my college studies. In the meantime, I hung out with the other models I knew from Phoenix who had also moved to the city that summer.

As new models, we were frequently invited out for dinner, and showcased among prospective clients. I recall one afternoon when the some of the staff members at my agency took a few of us out for drinks. One of the staff told us that the true sign of success, in our first six months in New York, would be having a man buy you a Rolex. This struck me as odd. At the time, I had no idea what a Rolex watch was. And I still can't understand why having a man buy me one would prove so significant.

One of my first modeling jobs that summer was for the cover of a romantic novel. I had just gotten dressed for the shoot, when a male model from another agency approached me. He looked at me in a way that I hadn't ever experienced before and told me how struck he was by my appearance in that dress. His gaze persisted throughout the shoot, and when we were finished he asked me if I wanted to share a cab back to midtown. As it turned out, he lived with a friend a mere two blocks from where I lived. While en route, he asked me out that evening. He took me to the neighborhood bar that his friend owned. It was a magical evening, the kind of evening I imagined most folks would associate with the city that never sleeps. Over the course of the next week or two, he often called me at the last minute to see if I wanted to go out. For a person who likes to plan things out in advance, this also struck me as odd. Yet, I wasn't from this city, he was, and I assumed that's the way things were done: on the spur of the moment. It was on one of those last minute dates when he introduced me to some of his family members. I assumed we were getting serious.

The next morning, I arrived at a catalog shoot to find two other models already in the dressing room. I listened as the young woman told the young man about her plans to move in with her boyfriend. When she mentioned his first name, my heart stopped. I knew that my boyfriend and this young woman's were one and the same. Nonetheless, I kept it to myself, posed for the photos with the two of them, and carried on like business as usual.

As soon as I got back to my apartment, I left a message for *our* boyfriend at his agency (as I didn't have his phone number). Within minutes, he returned my call. I told him whom I had met at my job that morning, and he pleaded: could he come over? He arrived shortly thereafter and confessed. Yes, it was true. She was his girlfriend and they had in fact planned to move in together. However, that had been before he had met me. Now, he wanted to break up with this other girl, that is, if he could move in with me instead.

I was devastated. Over the course of the following weeks, I tried to regain my composure and focus on my modeling assignments. The amount of work I was getting booked for continued to steadily increase, and the future seemed promising. Yet, internally I was reeling. The rug had once again been pulled out from under me.

On an evening in late October, I returned to my apartment after a dinner out with some friends. I mindlessly turned on the TV, paying little attention to whatever program was on. Yet, a television commercial advertising a brand of jeans soon captivated my attention. Set in a grade school classroom, the students danced about, displaying the logo on their jeans, as they waited for their teacher to arrive. The commercial moved me to tears. (Really, a jeans commercial moved me to tears? Yes really.) I knew what those tears signified. That commercial reminded me of where I truly belonged: in a classroom. At that moment, I knew what I needed to do: leave New York as soon as possible. And that is exactly what I did.

***

In the decades since, I have never regretted the decision I made that day. Yet, there were many who didn't understand it. Although I haven't modeled in over thirty years, I still have family members who refer to me as a model rather than an educator. From their perspective, that was the high water mark of achievement in my life.

So that leads to the questions I most want to ask that eighteen-year-old version of myself:

What, if anything, did she find life-giving in her work as a professional model?

And, if she had to do it all over again, that is—devote time and energy to a career in modeling, would she choose to do so?

What I most want to tell her is how I marvel at her courage. Somehow that eighteen year old girl had the self-assurance to abandon a path many young women fantasize about in order to claim her own.

She was resolute and unwilling to invest any more energy in maintaining external appearances or occupying environments that increased the likelihood that she would continue to be partially seen.

She refused to endure a life where her intellect and heart would often be overlooked. Mary hadn't done so, and neither would she.

Storytelling

Imagine meeting yourself at an earlier point in your life.

- What time in your life would you choose to return to and why?
- What question(s) would you most want to ask yourself?
- What would you most want to tell yourself?

What stories are you tired of hearing yourself tell?

There's one thing that you're probably going to need to sacrifice in order for this process to be really meaningful to you, something that you will have to give up. I'll tell you what that is: It's your story. Most of us have a story, or several stories, that we've been carrying around for a long time. In order to make this a meaningful process, you're going to have to recognize that story, and you will have to open up to that story being modified in some way. So, that story might have to do with your first marriage; that story might have to do with your childhood; it may even be a story about how hard your life is or how unfair your life is. I'm not suggesting that there isn't any truth to those stories. There probably is some truth to those stories. What I am suggesting is that they're not complete. Naikan gives you an opportunity to, essentially, create a story that's more complete and more accurate, reflecting on what actually happened in your life. If you're willing to let go of that story, or set it aside temporarily, you may find out that you'll come out with a very different story, or maybe not. We'll see.

—Gregg Krech,
Question Your Life: Naikan Self-Reflection and the
Transformation of Our Stories

I have been socialized to believe that life is a road. When you depart on a journey, have your destination in mind. As a little girl, I had a destination in mind: to be a teacher. And so I embarked on the road to that destination. I expected that the road would be like I-90 in

South Dakota. In spite of long stretches between exits, the road remains flat and straight; a driver can see miles ahead into the horizon.

I completed the required coursework and gained some experience teaching elementary students. As I did, I found that I wasn't energized working with children. I changed my major to secondary education, yet soon concluded that since I disliked high school, it didn't make much sense to teach in one. Yet, up to that point, I had never considered teaching at the college level. I hadn't known any academics personally and the few I had met while growing up were all men who seemed rather dull. Moreover, the grad students I had had as teachers at the university I attended looked chronically exhausted. It didn't seem an appealing way of life. Nonetheless, I so wanted to teach and teaching at the college level seemed to be the only option left for me. So once again I followed the map. I completed both a master's degree and a Ph.D. all the while firmly believing that with a doctorate in hand, I would be able to get a job teaching in a 4-year liberal arts college. I envisaged a campus in a beautiful location (perhaps on a hill somewhere). Ideally, it would be a Catholic institution like my beloved grade school. In that green, lush environment, students would flock to my office after class to reflect upon their lives and talk about what they were learning.

At the time I finished graduate school in 1992, hiring practices in higher education were beginning to shift. There was a glut of Ph.D.'s, an increasingly limited number of tenure-track job openings tailored for those who were highly specialized in a single discipline, and a plethora of adjunct teaching opportunities offering abysmal pay and no benefits. I was an interdisciplinary scholar who had intentionally aspired to keep my scholarship and teaching as broad as possible. I had no problem finding work as an adjunct instructor—that is, a road scholar. However, it wasn't finding a job I was after; it was finding a sense of place and a community of belonging.

As I entered mid-life, it was clear that the road I was on was not I-90. Ten years after the completion of my doctoral degree, I still hadn't arrived at what would have traditionally been the next destination on the road of higher ed: obtaining a tenure-track position. Instead, I had gone from semester to semester unsure of what my future employment status would be. My pay was embarrassing given the number of years of education I had completed and the number of hours I worked. Yet, the greatest source of my anguish was that, as an adjunct instructor, I felt peripheral to the institution. I didn't feel a sense of belonging.

I have often blamed myself for my predicament. For years, I lamented to myself that had it not been for my parents' divorce and the emotional turmoil that disrupted my life, I might have discovered my calling as scholar-teacher far earlier. I might have had far more confidence to pursue my graduate studies at a more prestigious school. I also might have been in less of a hurry to get married and start a family, and could then have relocated to where the tenure-track jobs were available.

Yet, I want to let go of that story in an effort to create a story that's more complete and more accurate. I want to look at the story of my professional life through a different lens. When I learned of Gregg Krech's work with stories using Naikan inquiry, I hoped that this approach might help me glean some new insights and discover new aspects of this story. [xix]

Naikan is a Japanese word that when poetically translated means "seeing oneself with the mind's eye." There are typically three questions participants are invited to reflect upon when they work with their stories using this approach (featured in italic print):

Were there ways that I was cared for and things I received that I'm leaving out of the understanding of the scene? Is there something I'm missing?

My husband has been my biggest professional advocate. The truth was: I didn't have to teach full time. Throughout our thirty plus years of marriage, he earned an income that could support our family. The other piece of my story that is missing is that I didn't want to teach full time. In fact, I was frightened at the prospect. Given what happened during my first year of graduate school, I developed an ulcer and a sinus infection, I learned that my body didn't do well under that amount of stress. And that was well before we had a child to care for. Trying to push myself into a conventional academic trajectory did not appear to be good for my physical or emotional health. Therefore, I preferred to teach only 2 courses a semester, and would have gladly consented to a protracted path to tenure. Yet, such arrangements were uncommon.

Were there ways that I helped or gave others that I haven't considered in my understanding of the scene? Is there something I'm missing?

I persisted in developing and teaching new courses that I had created and finding ways of funding them (for example, through grant money). I also continued in my commitment to mentoring and advising students even if I wasn't being remunerated for doing so. I remember one of my mentors commending me for how generous I was with my time. Another had nominated me for the faculty advisor of the year award. Even though I received the most votes from my colleagues, I couldn't be given the award as I wasn't tenured or on a tenure track (ugh!). I felt demoralized. When a colleague told me that I had *virtual tenure*, that is, I would be invited to teach there as long as I wanted to, I thought to myself: if that's the case, then why I am not being offered a tenure track position?

If I consider others who were part of the scene, can I see ways that I've caused them trouble or suffering? Can I try to understand their experience and what it was like dealing with me in that situation?

I'm not sure that I caused my colleagues trouble or suffering other than subjecting some of them to my broken record lament about my inability to move forward. I believe the person for whom I caused the most trouble and suffering was myself. I kept holding myself up to unrealistic standards by seeking out pathways that didn't exist in academic settings. Academic culture is not known for innovation. As a dear colleague once said to me, "Diane, it's not like the business world, they *don't create positions* here for talented people." And yet, since I had experienced that at the beginning of my teaching career, I had assumed it was only a matter of time. I just had to prove myself.
. .

So it's time to take that broken record off of the phonograph. It's not that I've failed; rather I had been aiming at the wrong target.

Here is the story I am learning to tell that is more complete and accurate. I noticed the shift in my story when I began writing. I was very aware of how I was still teaching, creating, and designing new courses through the books I wrote, yet I was able to control the cadence of activity rather than having a cadence imposed on me. Working as a writer, coupled with retreat work, professional speaking, and occasional classroom teaching has proven to be very life giving for me. While I still yearn for a professional place of belonging with an office and opportunities for daily interactions with students and colleagues, I am grateful for how the pieces of my professional life puzzle have coalesced. I hope that I have many more years of teaching, facilitating, and writing ahead of me, and I pray that I will continue to have fidelity to responding to the calling I hear. May I continue to listen even when, and especially when, the call that I hear doesn't resemble the plan I had in mind.

Storytelling

Think of a story that you are tired of hearing yourself tell. Consider:

- Were there ways that I was cared for and things I received that I'm leaving out of the understanding of the scene? Is there something I'm missing?
- Were there ways that I helped or gave others that I haven't considered in my understanding of the scene? Is there something I'm missing?
- If I consider others who were part of the scene, can I see ways that I've caused them trouble or suffering? Can I try to understand their experience and what it was like dealing with me in that situation?
- How do your responses to these questions help you to re-author your story?

What stories are you wrestling with how to tell?

Even as a mother protects with her life
Her child, her only child,
So with a boundless heart
Should one cherish all living beings;
Radiating kindness over the entire world …

— The Metta Sutta
(The Buddha's Words on Lovingkindness)

I had never realized the depths of love that one person can have for another until I became a parent. Soon after our son Ryan was born, the Buddha's words on lovingkindness became my spiritual practice. Walking through the aisles of the grocery store, juggling Ryan in my arms and my coupons in my hands, I tried to remember to look at the other shoppers as if they too were my beloved only child. While I often forgot to do so, or could only do so momentarily, I have continued to hold this aspiration over the course of the past twenty-five years: to cherish all living beings.

It was parenting that prompted me to cultivate a boundless heart, and it was parenting that pushed me to acknowledge that I am quite bounded.

At one level, parenting starkly showed me my limitations. I'll never forget how often I sighed audibly as I drove Ryan the 44-mile round trip to his Catholic school and back. I relished when it rained on the night of his soccer games, and even offered one time to pay him five dollars if he skipped going to karate (to save me the drive). I wanted to be *the cool mom* who hosted all the kids at the *go to house*, yet preparing food and entertaining big groups is not something I have ever done with ease.

At a deeper level, what I found most challenging about parenting is that it required me to return to childhood. I had found childhood something to be endured. I had disliked being relegated to the kids' table when the conversations at the adults' table seemed so much more interesting. I never understood the point of recess when the real action was what happened inside the classroom. I often wondered why anyone would prefer to be a kid and play with friends when as an adult, one could get married and go out to dinner instead. I had waited so long to be adult. And once I was finally there, I preferred to spend as much time as possible in the land of adults, or in my case, the land of young adults who filled my classrooms.

In sum, parenting forced me to mingle in situations that I would have never willingly chosen for myself: attending games, arranging play dates, and making small talk with other parents. I frequently felt ill equipped in these situations; they triggered my own discomfiture.

At the deepest level, parenting forced me to revisit a time in life to which I never wanted to return. The social terrain of middle school and high school had scared me as a girl and youth; middle school and high school *still scares me* as an adult. As a parent, it was doubly terrifying. I felt even more powerless as I was no longer living through it, I was witnessing someone I loved live through it: a boy who experienced being bullied and ostracized.

The fondest memories I hold of Ryan's middle and high school years were the parent teacher conferences. He had been blessed to have some truly remarkable teachers. It was one of those teachers who had told me how she hoped her own son would grow up to be like Ryan. After bestowing this touching compliment, she then lowered her voice and added, "I hope, for Ryan's sake, that you'll transfer him to a different school for high school. The group of boys in this eighth grade class is unusually cliquey. Many of them have known one another and played hockey together since grade school. And they have made no effort to get to know Ryan, all they've done is tease and belittle him."

If it was just about reading to your child, holding him in your arms and talking with him, or helping him with his homework, parenting would be a piece of cake.

Yet it's so much more.

It hurts to love someone that much, and it hurts to see someone you love so much being hurt.

I so wish I as a mother could have *protected with my life*

Him, my child, my only child,

From the pain he endured.

I often ask myself: what might I have done differently?

Had another child to ensure he would always have a companion? Perhaps, yet there are no guarantees that siblings will become best buds.

Arranged more play dates? Signed him up for more activities? No and no, we wanted our son to develop his own locus of control, not be beholden to ours.

Try to be more compassionate with myself, my bounded self, for the person I am and the parent I was? Yes and yes, that seems the most appropriate response.

Can I learn to acknowledge and tell the story of the growth that occurred in me as a result of being stretched in ways I would have never chosen to be stretched?

Can I learn to tell the story of how parenting has helped me cultivate more courage by witnessing my son's immense courage?

That is the story I most want to tell. Ryan was a young man who persisted in trying to keep his heart open to others, even when his life might have been far easier in the short term had he kept it shut. As much as I had hoped to teach him, guide him, and protect him, he is teaching me, guiding me, and perhaps protecting me from being too hard on myself.

This is the story about parenting that I hope to learn how to tell more fully.

Storytelling

- What aspects of your story are you currently grappling with how to tell more fully?

With whom would you most like to share your story?

"...in the Third Story there is no judgment about who is right or even whose view is more common. The Third Story simply captures the difference. That's what allows both sides to buy into the same description of the problem: each feels that their story is acknowledged as a legitimate part of the discussion.... You can begin from the Third Story by saying, 'My sense is that you and I see this situation differently. I'd like to share how I'm seeing it, and learn more about how you're seeing it.'"

—Douglas Stone, Bruce Patton, and Sheila Heen,
Difficult Conversations:
How to Discuss What Matters Most

Stone, Patton, and Heen implore us to begin from the standpoint of the Third Story—the recognition that there are at least two versions to the story of any relationship: ours and the other's. The Third Story is not so much a story; it is a stance rooted in curiosity, compassion and willingness.

- The first story: my version of the story;
- The second story: the other person's version of the story;
- The third story: including both versions of the story.

The first story: my version of the story.

My story is aided in large part by the framing of Alice Miller, in her book, *The Drama of the Gifted Child*. I read Miller's book in grad school and identified with the gifted child's way of being. Gifted children have the capacity to read what their parents need and in turn, do their best to supply it. (Don't all children?) Some parents are better able to focus on their children as opposed to expecting their children to fulfill their needs. So the gifted child learns to downplay his or her own needs and play up the parent's. The gifted child learns to notice what the parent needs from them rather than what the child needs from the parent. As a little girl, I tried to gain my father's attention by doing things that he enjoyed doing: watching Sunday football, playing gin rummy, and "working" at his dental office. My felt sense is that he was perpetually distracted; he was physically present, yet seemed psychologically absent. My favorite meal was fondue, as it required him to stay at the dinner table for more than five minutes.

Based upon what I know about my father's childhood, he too had been a gifted child: ever vigilant of his mother's needs. Throughout my childhood, I heard stories about the amount of time he had spent as a child helping his mother with housework and the care of his younger siblings. He often remarked: *If she had only had one child, she could have had a life. She shouldn't have had any more than two.*

She had seven. Her sixth baby, a little girl they named Betty Jo, (a combination of my grandmother's and grandfather's names), never made it home. Betty Jo died in an influenza epidemic that swept through the hospital's nursery. After that, my grandmother experienced a breakdown. It was up to my father, and my grandfather, to try to bring her back from wherever she had gone. My dad had told me the story only once—about how hard he and his dad had tried to revive her spirit and how helpless he had felt. After I heard that story, I often wondered: *was that the point at which he gave up the prospect of trying to revive anything or anyone?*

Yet, the preferred story my father liked to tell about that excruciating time in his family's life was the story of the music box. It was an Irish priest who had brought the music box as a gift for as my grandmother after Betty Jo's death (the fact that he was Irish is particularly significant as my grandmother's Irish roots were so often disparaged). The priest had placed the lovely wooden box in the living room, and it had never been moved after that day. Positioned in close proximity to her favorite chair, my grandmother could rest and listen to the music as it played. It was music that helped revive her spirit at a time when seemingly nothing else, or no one else, could.

I vividly remember that music box. It was the first thing I saw each time I entered the front door of my grandparent's house. Moreover, I remember what a special occasion it was when my grandmother would open up the box for us, and allow us to hear it play—as we children were not permitted to ever open the box on our own.

***

Begin with the third story: acknowledge that there are two versions of every story.

My version of the story is that over the course of my life, I've grown accustomed to having little to no expectations of my father. While he made arrangements to see us after our parents' divorce, once we became adults it was up to my sisters and me to visit him, and up to us to call him on special occasions and holidays.

Now, it is only on rare occasions that I feel the crush of grief. It happens unexpectedly, like the time at my son's school mass when I saw one of his classmates interacting with her grandfather. It was then that it hit me: I had never dared to imagine my father attending one of his events.

Yet, I know he wants to be acknowledged for the role he has played in our lives. My sisters and I dare not broach our disappointment in him; rather I often feel that it is we who have let him down.

I know he has his own version of this story to tell, and I hope that I will have an occasion to hear it while he is still living. I'd love nothing more than a redemptive ending to this story. You know the one: where the father shows up and reengages in such a way that the family forgets that he had ever been disengaged.

Yet, as wonderful and unrealistic as that might be, what I most want is *an occasion to tell him my own version of our story*, and that *he would be willing to hear it*. To date, I cannot recall a time, regardless of my age, when I could express my anger and disappointment in him to him.

Yet, my version of our story is not limited to a tale of anger and disappointment. While I may never know the second story, his version of their story, I will never forget....

. . . the tears in his eyes the day he brought my sister and me to his office and told us about his plans to see us after the divorce; and

. . . the tears in his eyes many years thereafter as we watched a slide show of pictures featuring me and my sisters with him during our visits after the divorce; and

. . . I will always remember the three music boxes he purchased and shipped to each of us less than a decade ago. Mine now sits right by the entrance to our home. It's one of the first things you see when you enter the door.

While I may never know why he disengaged as a father and grandfather, the gift of the music boxes signals for me a hope that our relationships with him may yet be revived, just like my grandmother's spirits were oh so many years ago.

Storytelling

- With whom would you most like to share your story and why?
- Regardless of whether or not you have the chance to tell them your version of the story in person, what would you like them to know?
- How do you imagine they would tell their version of the story?

Whose stories would you like to better understand?

That our stories—the stories of everyday people—are as interesting and important as the celebrity stories we're bombarded with by the media every minute of the day. That if we take the time to listen, we'll find wisdom, wonder, and poetry in the lives and stories of the people all around us. That we all want to know our lives have mattered and we won't ever be forgotten. That listening is an act of love.

Dave Isay,

Listening Is An Act of Love

"Have you ever told your story before?"

"No."

"Why not?"

"No one ever asked."

Dave Isay wanted to change that. In 2003, he set up a recording booth in Grand Central Station and launched the StoryCorps Project. Isay had learned, through his work as a documentary radio producer, that a microphone gives people permission to ask questions of others that they normally wouldn't ask. Since then, tens of thousands of people have been asked by a friend or family member to share their stories in one of the StoryCorps recording booths found throughout the country. Isay reflects in his book *Ties That Bind*, "We can discover the most profound and exquisite poetry in the words and stories of the noncelebrated people around us, if we just have the courage to ask meaningful questions and the patience to listen closely to the answers."[xx]

In the classes I teach on narrative, I invite my students to "enter the booth" with an interviewee of their choosing for 40-60 minutes. This may be a family member, a friend, or any person whose story they would like to learn more about. I encourage them to use this assignment as an excuse for engaging someone in a conversation they had been longing to have. After the interviews are conducted, I invite each student to report to the class what they discovered about themselves and the other through the interview exchange.

The following story told by Kyle Homstad illustrates the risk and vulnerability in asking another to share their story, the courage it takes to listen to the other's story with curiosity and a desire to learn, and the immense rewards of doing so.

***

During my journey through my many stories, Dr. Millis told our class about the wonder and truth in listening to somebody else's story. It is a loving action we can take—to be that mirror—to give someone the opportunity to see themselves through somebody else's non-judgmental eyes. Dr. Millis has taught me the value of opening up and listening deeply, so I knew that this "interview" would be something that I would benefit from as well. I wanted to learn about myself while I learned about another. I chose to interview my father.

Over the years, it has been harder and harder to relate to my father due to us diverging politically, spiritually, and me having less and less time to offer. Despite this, there is a strong foundation that had been laid in our relationship in my early childhood years. My father put me on/in the seat of anything motorized since I was a baby. We have great memories riding trails and streets (I always sat on the gas tank; you can't get away with anything like that these days!) My father used to let me sit in his lap and steer and shift the gears. I always held his tools (actually he still makes me do that), and I cheered him on at the drag strip. These times mean a lot because he fought hard for them. Much of my early childhood was spent living in the fallout of my parents' rather nasty divorce. Anyone who has ever had to "visit" one of their parents will know what I am talking about. My dad and I are not the "feely" types, and many of our strong emotions about these times go unacknowledged. When they go unacknowledged it can be easy to forget what is so special about our relationship—it can be easy to get lost in a harsh fight about something ultimately trivial. This interview was an opportunity to acknowledge the story we share and allow it to yield meaning in us for today.

Throughout my class with Dr. Millis I have been asked to search deeply and ask myself "what wants to be said?" My relationship with my father seemed to come up often. My center was telling me something important about where to begin looking for new meaning in my story. I asked him many questions about the past and questions that had to do with our relationship. I didn't want to beat around the bush and I didn't want to have such an intentional conversation while simultaneously having a hidden agenda. I told him about how our past keeps coming up in class and how I have come to realize that he is such an important part of who I am. I half expected this, but he began to ramble about his job and how it was funny that I was interviewing him because he was selected to be interviewed at work and there was this new program at work and…. This went on for about 15 minutes. I sat quietly and listened patiently without interrupting to let the side-track and its irrelevance sink in; I had just said some pretty heavy stuff. When he stopped I asked very directly if he wanted to have this conversation. He said yes. I showed him a picture of us, that I brought in to share with the class, and his face changed a bit. The first thing out of his mouth was, "I put in as much effort as humanly possible so that I could be a part of your life." I knew we'd be up pretty late.

My dad wanted to make sure that he was the father he never had. I asked him, "What is your favorite memory of me?" Driving around in the "Red Car" together (his prized 1972 Pontiac LeMans GTO pictured above), riding motorcycles together my whole life, snowmobiling together, and the countless hours spent in the car driving to and from my mother's house. He drove 4 hours a week to see me. Engine oil is the life-blood of the Homstad relationship. I asked him what his regrets were, and this is where the conversation got very interesting. He deliberated for a while on what a regret even was. On some level he regrets nothing because he is so proud of who I've become, and on the other there were a lot of mistakes along the way.

Ultimately, my dad says he has just failed to take risks in life. He failed to commit to various things. Sure, there were examples of this, but after everything we had just reminisced about I didn't see how that story about himself could hold any water.

He says the happiest moment of his life is the day I was born, and the saddest the day I was taken away. I asked him, "What are the three most important lessons you've learned in life?" *Long pause* "Always wear safety equipment." We haven't laughed that hard together in a long time. For a time when I was younger, my dad only got to see me for a couple of hours a few times a month at a center that hosted supervised visitation. My dad had kept some voicemail recordings I left him and he shared them with me. In the recording, I was telling him about my first day of Kindergarten, and I can be heard saying, "Whatever you wanted to call for, call me whenever you need to." At this point I recalled one of the only times I've ever seen my dad *really* cry. I was very upset and he was trying to explain to me why I had to leave... again. That was it though; I had to draw the line there. I don't think we were ready for that kind of emotional acknowledgment.

We then had dinner and also worked on my car. There's nothing more manly-Homstad than eating nothing but a plate-sized porterhouse steak for dinner and wrenching. While I was pulling the oil drain plug on my car I told him that used engine oil is probably my favorite smell (either that or Vanillaroma air fresheners from the Red Car). He worked at Valvoline for 17 years, and you never could quite get that smell off your hands. My eyes were a bit wet at that point, but he didn't see it because I was under the car.

That night I learned *a lot* about myself and a fair amount about him as well. I was *very* intentional when I saw him that day. He was gentler and more present than usual. I made sure I gave him no reason to "armor up," as Dr. Millis warned about. He has a lot more wisdom than I realized—a lot to share. He's as crass as ever and certainly still doesn't understand my view of life, spirituality, or politics. But, he is my dad. He has learned a lot of important lessons in our life together, and I am *a lot* like him. In light of his warnings, I am inspired to take more risks and continue to listen deeply. I am empowered to make strong commitments to myself and my wife. I am convinced more than ever of the Spirit and sacredness of conversations. We re-visited a better story about our past and he's helping me tell a better story about my present and my future. My father taught me about true love through his sacrifices. He could have hoarded his possessions and chosen comfort but he pursued a relationship instead. We had great times in the Red Car, but he eventually sold it to support us. He loved that car more than anything, but he let it go for something greater. A special vehicle is gone but our greasy hands are not. He helped me build my first motorcycle, and he spent countless hours on a car he gifted me (originally handed down from my great grandfather). This experience has turned emotional and spiritual confusion into inspiration and a renewed sense of what is "worth it" in life. When we finally do have that "good cry" that I know is eventually coming, I know we'll be crying tears of joy and hope and not ones of loss, regret, and pain.

***

I grin from ear to ear when I recall the morning Kyle told our class whom he had chosen to interview: his father. While I wasn't surprised with his choice, I marveled at his courage. Over the course of the semester, we had seen the picture of him and his dad in their red car, we had noticed a few tears fall on to his biker's leather jacket as he spoke about their relationship, and we had witnessed his yearning to reconnect with his father.

After class that day, Kyle came up and told me there was something he wanted me to hear. It was then that he played one of the voicemail messages his dad had saved from almost twenty years earlier. In it, we hear Kyle as a child telling his dad about his first day of kindergarten. In many ways, it was a seemingly ordinary message, and one that now held extraordinary meaning for him. Knowing that his dad had saved that message, and others of his, revealed a previously unseen storyline from which a new story about their relationship could now be told.

Storytelling

"Enter the booth" with an interviewee of your choosing for 40-60 minutes. This may be a family member, a friend, someone you have known for some time, or any person whose story you would like to learn more about. Prepare your list of questions and give them to your interviewee in advance of your conversation.[xxi]

Following your interview, consider:

- Whom did you most want to interview and why?
- What did you discover, through your interview, about yourself and the other person?
- What else, if anything, would you like others to know about your experience?

Whose stories break your heart?

Think globally but act locally. When my friends and pupils who want to help ask me what they should do, I always say the same thing: follow your heartbreak. Determine which one of all the causes in the world really breaks your heart. When you identify this, you have found the cause you will always have the energy and passion to work for. Once you have identified this cause, act immediately in your local community, so your heartbreak doesn't remain abstract but becomes a living force of practical compassion in your daily world.

—Andrew Harvey,
The Hope: A Guide to Sacred Activism

I'm no activist. Activists hold up signs, stand in picket lines, and yell out slogans. I've never held up a sign, stood in a picket line, or yelled out a slogan. Activists travel to impoverished places and go for days without showers. I have traveled to impoverished places, yet only as a tourist with a guide leading the way. Truth be told, the thought of going days without a shower unhinges me. I'm one of those people who heads to the nearest washroom after exchanging the sign of peace at church.

Yet I do know which one of the causes in the world really breaks my heart.

It's seeing the little girl, head wrapped in a hijab, standing on the perimeter of the playground. Her only companion: the tree that she stood underneath. As she watched her classmates run about, skip, jump, and swing, I watched her. In fact, my eyes were riveted to her

101

as I wondered: what is she thinking as she stands there? How is she feeling? What is it like to be her? And why is my attention so captivated by her?

It's hearing the news story about the Rohingya woman whose 4-month-old baby has no name. This 18-year-old mother, whose name and face had to be concealed to protect her identity, doesn't know what to call her daughter. Every time she holds the little girl, she says she is reminded of the violence that brought her daughter into being. She had been brutally raped repeatedly by six members of the Myanmar military forces last year. They not only stole her virginity. These troops murdered her mother and sister in front of her, then kidnapped her, and kept her for 10 days.

The stories that break my heart are about all those who are: Isolated. Unknown. Overlooked.

Is there anyone with whom this little girl can talk about her thoughts and feeling?

Is there anyone, other than the reporter, with whom this eighteen-year old mother can tell her story?

On every playground, there tend to be at least one or two children standing on the perimeter, just like in every community there are typically one or two people whose voices are never heard or whose presence is disregarded. And throughout the world, there are women and men living in situations and enduring conditions that I can scarcely imagine.

It breaks my heart to see anyone overlooked. My idea of heaven is a place where no one is isolated, and everyone is running, jumping, skipping, and swinging together.

In response to my heartbreak, my cause is cultivating attentiveness, that is, cultivating our capacity to look closely at, and listen deeply to, one another. And I can't think of a more important cause to address in an age where **we are no longer present to those in our presence.** We not only overlook people on the periphery; we overlook people in our proximity.

It breaks my heart to see parents gazing into their screens rather than into their child's eyes, entire families at the dinner table tethered to their devices rather than talking with one another, two people walking side-by-side texting rather than engaging with each other.

Yet there are notable exceptions. I'd love for you to meet my friend Natalie, a recent college graduate, who aspires to change the world one person at a time. When her mother asked Natalie why her new tattoo says "one person every day" she said it reminds her that while she can't eliminate poverty or eradicate all racial injustices in her lifetime, **she can be present to one person each day.**

While I'm not planning on getting a tattoo any time soon, Natalie's approach to activism helps me to see that maybe I am more of an activist than I realize. You see, the main reason I teach and write about topics such as the sacred art of conversation and deepening engagement is that I firmly believe we can transform and heal our world through the manner in which we encounter one another.

We live in a world where so many people are hurting. Yet, few of us showcase our struggles on our social media platforms, so where do we go to tend our hearts' deepest truths? Ideally, if Natalie and I have our way, we will turn to one another.

I invite you to give it a try. Take up Natalie's challenge. Set down your phone and turn to look closely and listen deeply to one person this day—a coworker, a family member, or someone with whom you've never spoken. Ask them how they are doing, and after you do, take the time to linger and listen to their response.

Storytelling

- Whose stories break your heart? Think of one or two examples to illustrate.
- How do their stories relate to your own experience of heartbreak?
- What cause for activism stems from your heartbreak?

What story captivated your attention today?

Many of us venture out into nature looking for signs of life with our cameras. We're moved by something as we shoot, unaware that there's more to the image than meets the eyes, that it contains, perhaps, an answer to a question, a clue for our life's journey.

—Jan Phillips,
God Is at Eye Level: Photography as a Healing Art

Gusts of wind assailed me that frigid December morning as I trekked through the woods in central Minnesota. A fallen tree soon caught my eye. Intrigued by how its branches were being held up by a neighboring tree, I considered photographing the intermingled trees. I reconsidered as soon as I heard a story surface. *I am both the fallen tree and the supporting tree . . . I am being invited to enter into this both/and way of seeing myself.* I knew full well that rehearsing a narrative in advance circumvented the deeper intent of the exercise: *to receive* a photograph and then *reflect upon the story* it is revealing to you. So I pressed on. Internal narratives continued to arise in tandem with the external sights. On the verge of giving up, I turned to head back to the retreat house. As I did, my eyes were drawn to a distant hillside filled with an odd assortment of orange and cream-colored tubes. In the midst of so much natural beauty, their garish appearance initially disturbed me until I got closer and discovered: there were saplings inside of those containers! I knew that this was to be *my one and only* picture for the day.

Earlier that morning, I had invited the retreat group I was facilitating to follow the pull of their heart—rather than the push of

105

their ego—as they discerned which single object or scene to photograph. Undoubtedly, I had experienced a felt sense of being pulled to that grove of orange and cream containers. My initial impression was that they offered an apt metaphor for my calling. Those cylinders protect the saplings from the fierce winds (and hungry deer), just as my mission as an educator has been to offer a protective container for those I teach and counsel. My aim is to provide a shelter for my students and retreat participants as they discern *the sound of the genuine* from all of the other sounds streaming through their environments.[xxii] Yet I suspected that there was an even deeper message that my photograph wanted to convey to me if I took the time to linger with it.

Back at the retreat house, I continued to gaze at the image I had photographed. Shortly thereafter something clicked: this wasn't just one sapling I was looking at; it was *a hillside full of saplings*. Whereas earlier in my teaching and ministry, I had felt it was incumbent *upon me* to provide a sheltering space for my students, this photo pointed to a new expression of the calling I am hearing: to accompany people within their communities as they *learn together how to provide shelter to one another.*

Yet, the revelation didn't end there. As a part of our retreat gathering, we each had a turn to share a story about what our photograph was revealing to us within a small group. (Specific guidelines are featured at the end of this chapter.) Each of us was given a heart-awakening question by the members of our group, a question that invited us to deepen our reflection about the story we had shared. Participants wrote their questions on index cards and took turns reading them out loud (before handing their index cards to the storyteller). Each of us was invited to choose only one question to respond to in the presence of the group. Responding to only one question permits movement into deeper interior reflection rather than the pressure to address them all.

Here are the questions I received from my small group that morning:

- How do you create a container for saplings?

- How would you honor or create ritual around the removal of the protective tubes?
- What are the tender, vulnerable shoots in you, and where will you look for community to help you strengthen and grow?
- What is your plan to protect more hillsides?

While I found all of these questions to be richly evocative, I selected the last one—about my plan to protect more hillsides. It was the question I found to be the most enlivening at that moment in time. I also sensed in responding to it in the presence of the group, it would help me further develop the story of my calling. Prior to this retreat day, I had been noticing a shift in my understanding of my calling. Over the course of my career, I had been invited to do more and more teaching outside of traditional classroom settings, which involved working with communities in a wide array of sectors. As I responded to the question, I noticed how much joy I heard in the tone of my voice as I described the wide array of communities in which I have had the privilege to serve and how emboldened I felt about the prospect of working with even more. I really like the challenge of working with stakeholders in various sectors to design meaningful learning experiences with the aim of deepening their engagement with each other. My job is to work with the saplings within their respective hillside to create habits and practices that strengthen their capacities to converse deeply with one another; trusting that some day they—these trees—would grow strong enough to engage deeply on their own.

Storytelling

Activity: To select an object or scene, and **only one**, to photograph. [xxiii] This exercise is designed to help us notice the difference between *taking* a photograph and *receiving* one, between being drawn and being driven, between the pull of our deepest self and the push of our ego. [xxiv]

Preparation: Allow yourself time to settle into stillness before embarking on your quest.

Close your eyes, turn your attention within, and breathe deeply. As you open your eyes, set your intention to open the lens of your heart.

Process:

Look closely at your environment. Notice the objects and scenes to which you are drawn, those that seem to *speak to you* and captivate your attention.

Listen deeply to your internal commentary—sensations, images, feelings, and thoughts—as you explore your environment. As you listen, notice which particular object or scene resonates most deeply for you (even though you may not understand why). Photograph that object or scene.

Linger intentionally with the image you have photographed. Consider....

- How does your picture connect with what is going on in your life at this time?
- What story is arising within you as you gaze upon your picture?

Now, bring your photograph and the story it is evoking in you to your next small group conversation. May the others' heart-awakening questions encourage you to listen more deeply to the story waiting to be told.

What is one of your most meaningful artifacts?

It is only with the heart that one can see rightly. What is essential is invisible to the eye.

—Antoine de Saint-Exupéry,
The Little Prince

It was the buzz in the room I remember most, the oohs and ahhs of the women as they looked at the dolls displayed on the table.

I was bemused.

I had almost turned around that morning and headed out the door after seeing the dolls. Why on earth would anyone devote an entire Saturday to doll making? This just wasn't my thing. Yet, what so many others find grounding—arts and crafts, cooking, gardening—I often find draining. Given the choice, I would much rather sit and read or sit and write than try to create things with my hands.

Yet here I was, looking at a table filled with fabrics, sequins, and accessories galore. Given my respect for the retreat facilitator and the other women from my parish with whom I had gathered in our church's basement meeting space, leaving wasn't an option. Instead, I came up with a strategy. I would:

— be a good sport;

— go through the motions of the day; and

— pitch the doll I had made in the trash can as soon as I got home.

111

We were instructed to begin by taking a small amount of wet clay to mold the doll's head. As the clay started drying and cracking, I was dismayed. Tricia, the retreat leader, had emphasized the guiding principle for designing one's doll:

Listen within at each step in the process and let your inner guide shape your unfolding creation.

Yet, my doll's cracked face seemed so ugly. I wondered: what on earth is my inner guide trying to convey to me?

Our next step was to choose the doll's hair. Since that just seemed like too much work, I decided that my doll was going to be bald. *Was it my inner guide that had prompted such a decision?* It must have been because a girly girl like me would never choose baldness over long hair and curls. Yet, after seeing the cracked face coupled with the baldhead, I *knew* that this doll wanted to be a man.

After the head and hair were complete, we were instructed to attach the doll's head to a bottle that served as its body. We would then paint the doll's face. Tricia suggested we begin with the eyes. However, as I began to paint the color around the pupil of the first eye, the paint smeared. So I had a choice: I could try to compensate for my error, cover it with white paint, and start again, or I could work with it. In a spirit of cooperation with my inner guide and what I might discover about myself, I worked with it. As the paint dried, the eyes took on a cloudy, milky appearance—like the eyes of someone who could not see. So now my doll was not only bald, he was blind.

The next to last step was to choose the doll's clothing. Finally, we had gotten to something I enjoyed. I carefully selected matching and coordinating colors, and chose fabric that would match the colors in my home—especially the sage color in our living room. Since I prefer to dress simplistically with little to no emphasis on accessories, I was surprised by how drawn I was to the large warm red heart resting on the table. *I knew* that this heart was the only accessory my bald and blind doll needed. However, placing the large warm red heart over the doll's sage fabric robe had a garish and disturbing effect on me. Instead, I nestled it underneath his garment; his large heart did not need to be visible to others.

Tricia then invited all of the retreat participants to bring their dolls with them into the adjacent candlelit room. She then guided us through an imagery meditation whose purpose was to discern a name for our doll. We were to listen deeply within for what our doll wanted to be named. This last step proved to be the easiest for me. His name emerged quickly and clearly. He would be called Trailblazer.

I felt emboldened as I gave my doll this name. In so doing, I was recognizing and claiming this doll's remarkable gift: he no longer had to depend on his outer senses to find his way in the world. His quest was to live from his heart and to see the world with the eyes of his heart.

***

Looking back at that day almost a decade later, I now see far more about what my inner guide was trying to convey to me through the creation of Trailblazer.

Trailblazer embodies my truest self. Like me, he yearns to look at others with the eyes of his heart AND to be seen. It's my large, warm heart that I most hope others will see.

So perhaps it goes without saying that Trailblazer never ended up in the trash. Heaven forbid! For the past ten years, he has been here at my side on the shelf in my office adjacent to my desk. While my eyesight has grown weaker since then, my capacity to see with the eyes of my heart has grown stronger. Unmatched by any other artifact I own, he exemplifies a way of being in the world to which I aspire. I can't imagine my life without him.

Trailblazer

Storytelling

- What is the story associated with one of your most meaningful artifacts?

Whose story helps you better understand your own?

It seemed, so great my happiness,
That I was blessed and could bless.

— W.B. Yeats,
The Winding Stair and Other Poems

We were nearing the end of the semester. Each Friday morning, as a part of our three-hour class meeting, students gathered in small groups for what came to be known as our 4-4-4 Storytelling Format. Through this process, each participant had:

- 4 minutes to tell a story in response to the guiding prompt;
- 4 minutes to receive questions and observations from their classmates; and
- 4 minutes to retell their story in light of what they had heard.

Over the course of the semester, I had noticed their tenderness with one another as they shared their stories. These seminary students were maestros of compassion, readily invested in hearing one another all the way to the depths of their stories as well acknowledging the beauty they found therein. Yet, it seemed that many, if not all of them, were struggling to see the beauty in their own stories. As the semester unfolded, I was heartened to hear more expressions of self-compassion being relayed in the stories participants told about their own lives.

For this class period, I had asked students to bring an artifact that held particular meaning for them and be prepared to share their story about it. Since our time was limited that morning, we met in dyads rather than in small groups. I also participated in the storytelling process so that each participant had a conversation partner. After counting off, Vicki and I were paired together.

We made our way to the adjacent prayer room. After we were seated, I asked Vicki if she would be willing to go first. Vicki nodded yes, reached into her folder, and took out two pieces of paper. I was struck by the great care with which she placed each page on the small coffee table nested between our two chairs. Through my eyes, it seemed as if Vicki were placing a paten on the altar.[xxv]

Vicki then began, "I have never shown these to anyone, yet I knew I was ready to show them to our class today. These are the two notes that my husband left for me before his suicide."

Over the course of the semester, Vicki had told the class about how she had lost her beloved husband, Glen, to suicide. She described how it had taken her over a month to find his body (which was eventually found in a storage locker he had rented). Here, on the opposite side of one of the two pages resting between us, was the receipt for the storage locker rental.

She continued, "I see so much love in these pages. I never questioned my husband's love for me, even after his suicide. I still don't. Yet, as I read these letters, I am reminded once again of his immense love."

Vicki then talked about how she felt called, as a chaplain in training, to work with families who had lost a loved one to suicide.

She emphasized, "I hope they too can grow to see how much their family member, who has died in this way, loved them."

Vicki paused and then looped back to talking about the love she had felt for her husband. In a previous class session, the class had witnessed her eyes fill with tears as she spoke of Glen as the great love of her life.

She then told me about the immense love they both shared for music. She asked me, "Did you know that he had been a professional musician?"

"Yes," I nodded, I had remembered that, "yet I don't recall what instrument he played."

At that moment, the sound of a trumpet began to play. Vicki looked in the direction from which the sound of music was coming, smiled and said, "the trumpet."

Vicki and I were speechless. We looked at each other. We looked at the two pieces of paper. We sat together quietly and listened as the trumpet played on.

After the trumpet playing stopped, we stepped into the hallway for a brief break. It was there that we met Dennis, a fellow student, holding the case containing his cherished artifact—a trumpet.

***

I often ask myself: What is being revealed here in the pages of the book of my life, especially those pages that continue to confound me?

And when I do, I now draw upon the story that Vicki told me that day and her observation, "there is love in those pages."

What struck me most about how Vicki told her story was the notable absence of self-pity. Losing someone to suicide would be one of the most difficult experiences to live through, let alone narrate in a redemptive way.

Vicki vividly embodied for me the wisdom found in the 14th century spiritual classic, *The Cloud of Unknowing:*

"Remember, dear friend, we live in a world that offers much in suffering, but also in consolation. You will not always understand it yourself, but seek to love it and seek to love yourself and to be loved. Know that the God of love has created us all, guides us all, and wills to bring us all back to Godself, the source whence we came."[xi]

Vicki really did see the love in those pages, and her example emboldens me to look for love—in all of Love's various guises—in more of the pages of my own life.

Moreover, our experience together reinforced my conviction that whenever two or three are gathered, there will be trumpet music playing in their midst.

Storytelling

- Whose stories have helped you to better understand your own?
- What specific lesson(s) did you learn from them?

Part Three:
Discerning the Stories Waiting to be Told

What is one of the days in your story of re-creation?

I Will Sing a New Song

The old song of my spirit has wearied itself out.
It has long ago been learned by heart.
It repeats itself over and over,
Bringing no added joy to my day or lift to my spirit.

I will sing a new song.
I must learn the new song for the new needs.
I must fashion new words born of all the new growth
*   of my life—of my mind—of my spirit.*
I must prepare for new melodies that have
*   never been mine before,*
That all that is within me may lift my voice unto God.
Therefore, I shall rejoice with each new day
And delight my spirit in each fresh unfolding.
I will sing, this day, a new song unto the Lord.

— Howard Thurman,
The Mood of Christmas

For years, I repeated a story over and over *that added no joy to my day or lift to my spirit*: the story about the phantom life I might have lived. I assumed that had I lived *that life* I wouldn't be dealing with the current difficulties in *this life*.

123

I wanted to learn how to *tell a new story for the new needs.* I wanted to *fashion new words that would open me to new growth.* I wanted to discern and learn how to tell my most life-giving story: the story I hear the Divine Author, my co-author, telling me about me.

After I discovered the above prayer, written by Howard Thurman (1899-1981), I prayed that I too would be given the grace to sing a new song. [xxvi] Rather than try to figure out how to sing a new song or tell a new story, I just kept offering my aspiration to do so in prayer.

Shortly thereafter, in 2016, I noticed a nudge. Pope Francis had designated that year as a Jubilee Year of Mercy, invoking the faithful to turn to God for compassionate love and mercy. I began reflecting and writing about where I sought greater mercy in my life: in my memories, in my relationships, in my view of myself. One night, I awoke and heard the following question arising in me:

If the mercy of God were woven into the fabric of creation, then wouldn't it make sense to tell my story of mercy akin to the story of creation, that is, in seven days?

So the next day, I officially began a writing project I entitled: *Seven Days of Mercy.* Through my writing, I sought to examine the events from 7 days in my life for which I sought greater mercy, insight, and healing.

Although I had no idea at the time, this endeavor proved to be one of the most fascinating writing exercises I have undertaken. While I had no intention of ever publishing the 7 Days of Mercy, and still don't, I knew that it had to be written. It was an assignment, a divine download if you will, that I had been given.

There were many days from my life that contended to be featured among the seven. The question then became:

Which 7 days would I choose and why would I choose those particular 7?

In truth, it required discernment, that is, ferreting out which events over the course of my life were asking for greater attention.

There were events from certain days that, after I began writing about them, lost their charge; I found there wasn't enough juice in them to write anything further. Nonetheless, there had been great value in writing about the events from all the days that I did, no matter how much or how little I had to explore.

I finished the 7 Days well before the Year of Mercy had ended, and after doing so, I felt as if something had been released in me. I found that through this prayerful writing, my compassion for my own story and myself had grown.

Two years later, as I began writing this book, or rather as this book began writing me, I noticed how some of the stories I had written about in the *Days of Mercy* were reappearing in this book.

So I wondered: would readers of this book find as much value as I had in experimenting with writing about seven days from their own lives?

***

Passive receptivity is the best attitude to adopt. Let the cycles of your life present themselves.

—Ira Progroff, At a Journal Workshop

Ira Progroff, a psychologist, developed an entire curriculum for exploring our life's story "through passive receptivity." In the workshops he offered, Progroff encouraged participants to relax their minds and just notice the memories as they emerged.[xxvii]

That is the very attitude I hope you will adopt for this exercise as well. Follow the trail of your life experience and notice the memories that arise to meet you.

Storytelling

So now it is your turn to give it a try. I invite you to discern:

- Which day from your life would you like to explore further in an effort to re-create the story you are telling about it?

- You may find that after exploring one day, you would like to continue and create your own writing project: Your 7 Days of Re-Creation.

- If you do, don't be concerned about choosing 7 days that represent the arc of your life span (for example, one day per decade). All seven days could be recent, or all seven may be from your distant past. Impose no restrictions other than to limit your selection to 7, acknowledging that the stories told about those seven days will organically interconnect with memories from other days.

What is the story of your best possible future self?

Think about your life in the future and write about this life as if you have worked hard and succeeded at accomplishing all of your life goals.

It is recommended that you devote fifteen minutes to writing your response to this prompt for four consecutive days.

— James Pennebaker and Joshua Smyth,
Opening Up by Writing It Down

For decades, the psychologist James Pennebaker has been examining the role of expressive writing and its potential healing benefits for working with traumatic memories. Pennebaker and his team have found that fifteen minutes of writing per day is the *just right* amount of time for an expressive writing exercise—not too much and not too little. Moreover, he has also found that to write for fifteen minutes for four consecutive days deepens the inquiry. However, not everyone who writes for fifteen minutes over four consecutive days reports a greater sense of well-being; the key is *how one approaches* what one writes about.

Pennebaker has found that those participants who examine the thoughts and feelings they had at the time the traumatic experience occurred, compared with the thoughts and feelings they have now about what occurred, report the greatest healing. It's important to note that while most participants report feeling sadder immediately following the writing; after a few days, they report an increased sense of ease and well-being.

I've been intrigued with Pennebaker's findings, and wanted to try them out for myself. He has found that 4 consecutive days of writing, for 15 minutes each day, proves beneficial for working with experiences of trauma and loss as well as for exploring one's deepest aspirations in life. Regardless of how busy we are, most of us can carve out fifteen minutes to experiment with this practice. I suspect that you, like me, will be amazed at how much one can get on to the page in such a small amount of time. I also noticed how after four consecutive days of writing, I felt as if I had exhausted what I had to say (at least for now).

So what did I discover through writing about the story of my best possible self?

My first day of writing focused a lot on outcomes. It consisted of bullet points featuring a combination of my bucket list and things I hope to contribute through my work. On day two, my emphasis shifted from what I aspired to do to who I aspired to be. This emphasis on identifying the way of being I hope to bring to our world persisted throughout my remaining days of writing. By day four, it crystallized in my consciousness as I kept hearing the lines from one of my favorite poems echoing within me:

To A Visionary Whose Name I'll Never Know

This is to you, lady who smiled at me
as I came out of the subway at 14th Street

and walked down 6th Avenue in the winter of '74
having just arrived in New York. Gentle feathers

of snow had just begun falling from the black.
I felt myself taken into your eyes, and suddenly

was no longer a confused young man
wondering whether every next step was the right one,

but a light-being, love built into his cells,
leaning forward, poised to give.

Thirty-five years later
I still walk those tunnels of your eyes

down the line of your smile
toward that person you saw in me.

— Max Reif [xxviii]

More than anything I have written or read, this poem captures the essence of who I aspire to be. Envisaging my best possible self, I hope to become more like what he, the poet, saw this woman to be—a visionary. I want to learn how to turn my full attention to more of the people I meet. I want to learn how to really see them, not categorically (*a confused young man*) but compassionately (*a light being, love built into his cells.... poised to give*).

The visionary Max Reif writes about in this poem embodies the values that have shaped me from my Judeo-Christian faith tradition. As Rabbi Arthur Green implores, in his *Ehyeh: A Kabbalah for Tomorrow:*

"Recognize every person as the image of God. Work to see the Divine image especially in those who themselves seem oblivious to it. Seek out the divinity in those you annoy, anger, or frustrate you. Hope to find and uplift sparks of holy light, even when it seems hardest. Do all the work that is needed to help others to discover the image of God in themselves."[xxix]

I want to increase my capacity to find and uplift sparks of holy light in more of the people that I meet, especially those whose spark may be dim or difficult to see.

And, I want to learn how to call out their beauty, as Jesus did:

"Unless we look at a person and see the beauty there is in this person, we can contribute nothing to him. One does not help a person by discerning what is wrong, what is ugly, what is distorted. Christ looked at everyone he met, at the prostitute, at the thief, and saw the beauty hidden there. Perhaps it was distorted, perhaps damaged, but it was beauty nonetheless, and what he did was to call out this beauty."[xxx]

***

The visionary woman archetype also exemplifies the values that have undergirded my approach to teaching and scholarship—that of a super-encounterer. It was Sandra Erdelez, an information scientist, who coined this term to describe her research findings regarding how people engaged with sources of unexpected inspiration and guidance. She found that people fell into three groups:

- "Non-encounterers"—those persons who stuck to their to-do lists and kept a tight focus;
- "Occasional encounterers"—those folks who every so often stumbled upon guidance from unexpected places or sources, yet didn't seek it; and

- "Super-encounterers"—those who believed they would find treasures even in the oddest places, (for example, a Victorian journal on cattle breeding) and as a result found insights everywhere.

"You become a super-encounterer," according to Dr. Erdelez, "in part because you believe that you are one — it helps to assume that you possess special powers of perception, like an invisible set of antennas, that will lead you to clues."[xxxi] As I read Erdelez's findings about how people engaged, or failed to engage, with unexpected sources of information, my mind quickly turns to a potential corollary: how might these ways of engaging with information also apply to how we engage with one another? That is, are some of us:

- Non-encounterers, tending to stick to the people we already know?
- Occasional encounterers, willing to open ourselves every so often to what we might learn from unexpected persons?
- Super-encounterers, aspiring to learn something from everyone we meet?

Undoubtedly, the visionary woman in Reif's poem is a super-encounterer. My best possible self follows her lead: fully focusing on the present moment, the ground where she is standing, and the young man she met there. She looked beyond his appearance into the depths of his being. It is as if she possessed Superman's heat vision and had the capacity to melt the shell casings in which his divine sparks were imprisoned. He felt seen, and in being seen, his beauty was revealed.

So returning to the questions we addressed earlier, who is the protagonist in the story of our best possible self?

What is your protagonist's name and why was that name given?

Visionary Woman. She aspires to look closely at more of the people she meets, to find and uplift their holy sparks, to call out their beauty, to learn from them, especially those that seem least likely to have something to teach her. She aspires to look beyond others' surface appearance, and acknowledge the depth in the other especially when it isn't readily apparent. She refuses to settle for first impressions, and remains willing to look again, and again. Most importantly, she aspires to remind those she meets of their inherent loveliness especially those who no longer recognize it in themselves.

What has she found life-giving?

Learning about prayer and the inner life, reading, writing, studying, teaching, facilitating, and sharing in-depth conversations with others.

How has she overcome or met her limitations?

She has developed greater compassion for herself, realizing that life is not about attaining perfection, it's about cultivating attention: attention to the particular ways in which she has been wounded; attention to her deepest desires; attention to the goodness, truth, and beauty woven into the fabric of creation, and waiting to be found both within her own and others' hearts.

What does she choose to highlight in her life story?

Her fidelity, her willingness to keep stepping out on to life's stage just as she did when she was a little girl, even if and especially when

132

she doesn't receive the response she initially anticipated. She chooses to highlight her courage and how she has persisted in stepping on to the stage of life with an open heart, taking the next step, pressing on, and enduring even when it's so damn difficult to live this way.

Storytelling

- What is your protagonist's name and why was that name given?
- What has your protagonist found life giving?
- How has your protagonist overcome or met her or his limitations?
- What does your protagonist choose to highlight in her or his life story?

What is your life story in six words?

I have arrived. I am home.

—Thich Nhat Hanh

In my imagination, I visited there often. Yet, it had been decades since I had actually set foot in the place. And as I did, I felt a wave of energy welcoming me home.

I ambled up the aisle to the center of the church, and slowly turned to take it all in. Although the altar had been remodeled since my last visit; the pews remained the same. I looked over at the pew where I, as a second grader, had sat on that memorable day—the first time I had ever attended mass on my own. I remember how grown up I felt walking unescorted from my classroom through the underground tunnel to the church. I relished being the only child gathered among the adults. Yet, the highlight of that experience was what had happened as I knelt in prayer before the mass started. It was then that I lost track of space and time. I entered into another realm of consciousness that I later learned was called a unitive experience.

I then looked at the lectern and recalled how I loved nothing more than being selected to read one of the scriptures or prayer petitions at mass. That little girl would have been thrilled at the prospect that over forty years later, she would be back offering a Lenten retreat for the women of this parish, her grade school parish. This was the realization of one of my life's dreams. I had always hoped that I would be invited to share my professional gifts as an educator at the place that had proved so foundational in shaping me. It was a return that I yearned to make.

Returning to that space helped me *remember* the desires I had held, as I looked at my life through her eyes. In many ways, I had done what that little girl had most wanted. I had become a teacher. I had moved to Minneapolis. I had attended the University of Minnesota. I had gotten married. I had had a child of my own. Moreover, there had been so many unexpected surprises in my vocational unfolding. She would have been amazed to know that someday she would teach at Catholic colleges and universities, and oh so relieved and grateful that her child would be able to attend a Catholic school from pre-K to 12 (something she had wanted to do, but her mother couldn't afford). Seeing my life through that little girl's eyes helped to assuage the professional disappointments I was carrying. I felt as if she was gently reminding me that it had never been my intention to be an "academic." I had done what I had most wanted to do. I had become a teacher, and I was teaching my life's curriculum.

In 1973, the year that I had moved away, the principal of the school, Sister Bernadine, had given me a gift: Antoine de Saint-Exupéry's book *The Little Prince*. Sister must have known that this little prince would comfort me, as he had the pilot. I too had often felt that I had landed on an unknown planet (during my time living in Phoenix). I smiled at the irony of it all. Sister would have been thrilled to know that it was one of the most oft-quoted lines from that book, *It is only with the heart that one can see rightly*, that I was now here to teach about. The brochure read:

"Seeing with the Eyes of Our Heart, Listening with the Ear of Our Heart

In this year's 2016 Lenten retreat, our presenter Dr. Diane Millis will show us how to go beyond the surface of things in order to more deeply engage in our interactions with one another. Together, we will explore ways to cultivate our capacity to see with the eyes of our heart, listen with the ear of our heart, and bring this heart-focused presence into more of our everyday conversations. Her presentation will draw upon specific themes from her books *Deepening Engagement* and *Conversation—The Sacred Art*. Please join us!"

During the retreat, there were moments when it all felt a bit surreal, especially as I read the Scripture readings at the morning mass, as well as signed books and talked one-to-one with the women who attended. There were moments when I felt as if my grade school self was looking upon us all with such great delight.

After the retreat, I took Mark on a pilgrimage to all my favorite sights in the Fargo-Moorhead area. We went back and saw both of the homes I had lived in while there, visited where my dad's dental office had been, walked in a park along the Red River, and shared a lovely dinner at a new restaurant in Fargo. It couldn't have been a more wonderful weekend, and before we headed back to Minneapolis, we returned to St Joseph's Church one more time for Sunday mass.

As we walked from the parking lot to the church that morning, I noticed right away that the area appeared different to me. I no longer saw the scene through my childhood eyes; I now saw it through my fifty-three year old eyes. My body had finally caught up with real time.

We entered the worship space, and I led Mark to the same pew where I used to sit with my family as a girl. After we genuflected and knelt to pray, the shift became more apparent. Although I was the same person in the same place, I was no longer spellbound by this place, rather *I was grateful for its place in my life.*

After mass, Mark and I stopped to have breakfast just as my family and I had done every Sunday when I was a girl. Yet, once we finished eating, I had no desire to linger. For the first time in my life, I was ready to leave Moorhead. It was now <u>my</u> choice to leave.

I was eager to get home, yet this time returning home meant heading East on Interstate 94 toward Minneapolis. However, at that moment, it really wouldn't have mattered which direction we headed on the interstate.

I had arrived. I was now at home with myself.

Storytelling

- *I have arrived. I am home.* These six words, attributed to Thich Nhat Hanh, concisely convey the story I am currently telling myself.
- What six words convey your current life story? [xxxii]
- How do these six words highlight what is most significant for you in your story?

Part Four:
Hearing Into Speech One Another's
Stories

Hearing to Speech

Hearing to speech is never one-sided. Once a person is heard to speech she becomes a hearing person.

—Nelle Morton,
The Journey Is Home

"It was in 1971 that I received a totally new understanding of hearing," Nelle Morton declared in her classic—*The Journey Is Home*. "It came from the lips of a most ordinary woman in a workshop I was conducting."

Morton describes how she first discovered the power that a community can play in helping us give voice to our most life-giving story:

"The last day of the workshop, the woman, whose name I do not know, wandered off alone. As we gathered sometime later in small groups she started to talk in a hesitant, almost awkward manner. 'I hurt,' she began. 'I hurt all over.' She touched herself in various places before she added, 'but I don't know where to begin to cry. I don't know how to cry.' Hesitatingly she began to talk. Then she talked more and more. Her story took on fantastic coherence. When she reached a point of the most excruciating pain, no one moved. No one interrupted her. No one rushed to comfort her. No one cut her experience short. We simply sat. We sat in a powerful silence. The women clustered about the weeping one went with her to the deepest part of her life as if something so sacred was taking place they did not withdraw their presence or mar its visibility. Finally the woman, whose name I did not know, finished speaking. Tears flowed from her eyes in all directions. She spoke again: 'You heard me. You heard me all the way.' Her eyes narrowed, then moved around the group again slowly as she said: 'I have a strange feeling you heard me before I started. You heard me to my own story. You heard me to my own speech.'"xxxiii

The story of the woman, whose name we do not know, and those who accompanied her provides a guiding archetype for all of us who yearn to learn to tell our most life-giving story.

As the women who so skillfully accompanied the unknown woman modeled for us, when someone connects with the essence of his or her own story: we don't move. We don't interrupt. We don't rush to comfort. We don't cut their experience short. We simply sit. We sit in silence.

Unlike the prevalent norms of so many social media platforms, the measure of a well-told story is not the number of likes, thumbs ups, or positive emojis it receives. The measure of a well-told story is the extent to which we as speakers convey the truest, most authentic story we can tell at this moment in time about our lived experience. Although it may not be a pretty story, a tidy story, or an easy story to tell, I believe **we can learn to tell our stories beautifully if we have listeners who create the conditions to hear us into speech.**

They include:

- A covenant, a set of agreements, regarding the ground rules to which conversation participants will hold one another accountable (see Appendix One);

- A structured process where every participant is given the same amounts of time to both speak and be heard (see Appendix Two);
- A commitment to practice deep listening (see Appendix Three).

The divine tuning fork of the human soul knows when it's in the presence of those who can accompany it to its own depths. And it also knows when it's not.

Hearing others all the way to their own story requires that we continue plunging courageously into our own. We can only accompany people as far as we ourselves have gone. We can only bear witness to the joy and suffering that we ourselves can both allow and feel all the way through.

Inspired by the example of the woman whose name we will never know and those unnamed few who accompanied her, may we vow to enter as they did into the precious depths of our own lives. May we vow to accompany others into the precious depths of theirs. And as we do, may we vow to discover that these depths are not separate, and that we are all, together, made new.

Offering a Space To Listen With Attention and Care

We cannot change the world by a new plan, project or idea; we cannot even change other people by our convictions, stories, advice and proposals; but we can offer a space where people are encouraged to disarm themselves, to lay aside their occupations and pre-occupations, and to listen with attention and care to the voices speaking in their own center.

—Henri Nouwen,
Reaching Out:
The Three Movements of the Spiritual Life

It is a precious gift to gather with one or more persons who help us increase our awareness of the life-giving aspects of our stories we may otherwise miss. Those who convey **what they noticed in us and in themselves as we told our story, what they appreciated and learned from the stories we shared, and the questions they wondered about as they listened.** In so doing, our companions won't allow us to settle for thin narratives, but encourage us to continue to listen for the incarnate and enigmatic expression of the Holy whose meaning isn't readily apparent and continues to be revealed over time. They invite us to consider alternative ways of naming and narrating how Mystery is at work in the stories we tell.

Noticing

The practice of *lectio divina*, or divine reading of a sacred text, invites us to pay attention to what stirs our heart as we listen to a sacred text being read. What word, phrase, or image seems to be speaking to us as we listen? In a kindred manner, we are invited to **pay attention to what stirs in our heart** as we listen to the sacred text of a person's story, and to **note what seems to stir their heart** as they speak. We notice the points at which . . .

- Their voice may get very soft as they struggle to find the words to convey what they want to say;
- Their voice may get very animated as they proclaim their enthusiasm and joy;
- Their eyes may begin to moisten or fill with tears;
- They may look off into the distance as if searching for what to say next;
- They may sign audibly or take a deep breath;
- They may speak more slowly and deliberately;
- They may emphasize and/or repeat a particular word or phrase.

Any of these behaviors offer us clues that something is stirring in the speaker; they may be entering uncharted terrain in their story or recognizing a forgotten truth.

As listeners, we too pay attention to those same movements in ourselves. At what points in the other's story did our heart feel stirred, enlivened, or anguished?

Appreciating

Any person's story can offer a portal into our own. When someone entrusts their story to us with candor, concreteness, and courage, when someone speaks from the depths of their heart, we can't help but see our own stories in a new light.

As we express our appreciation, we do not turn the attention from their story to our own. Rather, we aim to convey **the specific features** in their story **we found ourselves most drawn to** as well as **the ways in which their story illuminates our own.** For example,

- I appreciated your willingness to sign up for music lessons at this point in your life. Even though your family couldn't afford them when you were a child, you reminded me that it's never too late to pursue your interests.
- I appreciated your courage in deliberately engaging customers who complain. I marveled at how you moved toward rather than away from them. I hope I have the courage to try that the next time I hear someone complaining.
- I appreciated your willingness to continue working with your dreams, even though you often feel as if you have no idea how to interpret them. You motivate me to keep wrestling with my own dreams each morning, instead of rushing to get to my to-do list.
- I appreciated how much time you were willing to share with your neighbors, even though they may never thank you for doing so. You focused on the joy you receive in reaching out to others. It made me think: How might I shift my focus to joy rather than let my resentment fester?

Wondering

Our mind's natural tendency is to judge and assess as we listen. We often outstrip the rate at which a story is being told, as we think to ourselves: "I've heard this type of story before . . ." or "Here he goes again, telling me about his golden days . . ." We assume we know where the story is going, and its inevitable conclusion. As a result, we don't listen in real time for what is being revealed.

How would we listen if we actually believed that something new was being revealed in each and every story we hear?

We would turn to wonder. We would pay attention to the questions that arose in our hearts as we listen to the other's story, particularly those questions to which we do not know the answer. We would offer our questions to the speaker, trusting that through the gift of our questions they may discover something more in their story.

Too often the questions we ask are just another form of telling. They include thinly veiled advice or reflect our assumptions. However with practice, we learn the difference between asking a conventional question and offering a contemplative question. For example:

Instead of, *I wondered if it was awkward for you to share your story as you mentioned you'd never done this before.*

Try: *I wondered what it felt like to share your story with us today. You mentioned this was the first time you had ever done anything like this. What was this experience like for you?*

Instead of, *I wondered if you've ever tried journaling about this experience or bringing it to prayer.*

150

Try: *I wondered, as you reexamine this experience, would you prefer a do-over, a freeze-frame, to fast forward or some other approach?*

Instead of, *I wondered if you sought the assistance of a therapist.*

Try: *I wondered what you found to be the great sources of support during that challenging time.*

Our aim, as Henri Nouwen underscores, is to invite the speaker "to listen with attention and care to the voices speaking in their own center."

Therefore, as we listen, we discern: What can I ask this person, in such a way, that will help them listen more deeply within and give voice to more of their story?

***

The 4, 4, 4 Process
for
Hearing into Speech

"I can't believe how much I can learn about my story in as little as fifteen minutes," a participant exclaimed at the conclusion of her turn. It's not the first time I've heard someone offer this observation, and I know it won't be the last. For over a decade, I have been experimenting with formats for inviting participants in communities of small groups to *hear into speech* one another's stories. I have found that the 4, 4, 4 process provides safety, ease, and accessibility for groups of all ages and backgrounds.

What is the 4, 4, 4 Storytelling Process?

Telling: The focus person shares their story in response to one of the questions featured in this book | **Up to 4 minutes**

Responding: Listeners take turns contributing their responses to the story | **Up to 4 minutes**

    I noticed…

    I appreciated…

    I wondered…

Retelling: The focus person describes what s/he is discovering about her or his story | **Up to 4 minutes**

Pausing: Participants share time in silence to honor what has been shared | **Up to 1 minute**

It is a highly structured process, and it is the structure that cultivates safety, freedom, and ease.[xxxiv] Each person has the same amount of time to speak without cross talk, receive others' responses, and re-tell their story in light of others' responses. Allocating the same amount of time for every participant alleviates the concern that some participants may dominate the conversation while leaving others with little to no time to share their own story.

Another reason the 4, 4, 4 format has proven so powerful is it immediately requires the storyteller **to be selective in what they tell.** Having a clear time limit to which all persons will be held accountable to increases the likelihood that participants will speak more mindfully (and they do!). While having such a limited time may initially increase the storyteller's anxiety, that anxiety can be addressed by allocating time for participants to reflect in writing together before they share as a group or giving them the narrative prompt before their next meeting.[xxxv]

One of the most frequently asked questions is: what if someone doesn't speak for the entire four minutes?

It's a great question, as I have found that individuals who are sharing their stories for the first time tend to speak for about two to two and a half minutes.

It raises another related question: what should the group do with the remaining time? And we recommend: continue to sit silently and patiently with the person; *it's their time* whether they choose to fill it with words, or whether they choose to reflect on their story internally. More often than not, folks tend to add a bit more in the remaining time if others continue to hold the space for them to do so.

Yet it seems so awkward to just sit there in silence.

And it can be. Yet, there is much we as individuals, and as a group, can discover as we learn to embrace this countercultural way of gathering together. As Robert Sardello observes, in his book *Silence: The Mystery of Wholeness*:

"A first entry into the Silence between ourselves and others is to appreciate the pause, the stumbling, the inarticulateness, the gaps, and the searching that accompany speaking. These 'holes' in our speaking are not themselves the bearers of Silence, but they are foyers within which we are able to listen for the approach of Silence, for the beckoning of the ineffable. Listening is required for the soul of speech to live, a listening that does not come only before or after we speak but within our speaking itself. This special kind of listening waits patiently, without the need to fill in any emptiness. We can easily feel when we are speaking in this manner rather than conveying information or letting the chatter in our mind spill out endlessly."[xxxvi]

Being in the company of those who can appreciate our pauses, rather than rushing to fill them, is an immense blessing. Their palpable presence empowers us to linger intentionally, and notice what arises in our hearts—which may or may not take the form of words.

Silence is a foundational practice for any meaningful conversation. When we pause together in silence, we learn that our ability to be present to one another doesn't always depend upon words. We remember that the deepest level of communication is beyond words; it is an invitation to communion.

The 4, 4, 4 Process:
An Illustration

Listening requires the discipline of very few words and enormous patience to penetrate the great clouds of ambiguity while living in them. People talk at and then around things, and they go around and around again. So many things are said and then repeated ... Anger, bitterness, regret, sadness, loss, and misunderstanding are all mixed in a bundle of messages made up of words and images, spoken and unspoken. In the midst of that very human mess, listening is the art of connecting and finding the essence.

—John Paul Lederach,
The Moral Imagination:
The Art and Soul of Building Peace

Since we learn to tell our most life-giving story in the company of one of more committed listeners, my hope is that you will explore this book's guiding questions in conversation with others.

Below you will find the story of one small group's experience: three listeners who accompanied a storyteller as she responded to the prompt featured on page 42: **Who is the protagonist in your story?**.

The storyteller tells her story in the third person (which is how I recommended participants respond to this prompt).

Telling: The focus person shares their response to a story prompt | Up to 4 minutes

Sister Elise began: The name of the protagonist in my story is Twin.

Twin has found that being a twin is very life-giving for her. She has always had a friend. Her sister was her perpetual playmate and shared the same interests as Twin. The twins loved especially to play with their dollhouse and schoolhouse and also with their paper dolls. Through this play they re-enacted what they loved most – being part of a Catholic parish, attending school with friends and being involved in church activities, and being part of a closely-knit family with strong connections to nearby relatives. As they grew older, the two girls shared deeply about their ambitions and dreams. They took long walks and talked for hours. Although her sister had first expressed the idea of becoming a Sister, because a teacher had told her that she possibly had a religious vocation, Twin felt within herself a deep love for Jesus, stemming from her First Communion Day, and a desire to serve the Church as a teacher. Nobody really affirmed that call.

In the midst of all the life-giving experiences, Twin often felt confined. She referred to herself as a shadow or a tag-along. She knew herself to be either half a person or a double person. The sisters had to dress alike, sit together in school, and were expected to take the same courses in high school and pursue the same path in life. Having been born second, Twin slipped into the role of being a follower. She watched her sister have the lead in the second grade class play, be voted the most popular student in the eighth grade class, and win an award in a Constitution contest in high school. Several years later, when both young women were preparing to enter the convent, Twin's mother insisted that the only reason Twin was doing this was because her sister always dominated her and had talked her into it. On the day they actually entered the convent, Twin purposely passed by the family as they walked up the front sidewalk and opened the door of the convent and stepped inside ahead of her sister. Twin knew what was deep in her own heart.

After four years in the convent, Twin's sister left religious life. The consecrated life was not a fit for her. She eventually got married and gave birth to five children. Family and relatives often gathered at her home for holidays and special events in the children's lives. Twin watched as her sister received much admiration and praise for her cooking, her accomplishments, and the gifts of her children. On these occasions Twin felt comfortable in the kitchen, cleaning up after the meal and doing the dishes with her mother. She was not aware of the hole in her heart.

Twin had a deep need to be affirmed and recognized. Her lifestyle needed to be validated, for in truth, she dearly loved religious life and was convinced that she did indeed have a personal call from the Lord. Twin needed to be recognized for her own accomplishments as a teacher and a director of religious education. She would have been so happy if her family would have shown an interest in her ministry and would have asked her some questions about it. Family members and relatives seemed delighted to see her, but except for her mother, were very satisfied to just let her be.

And then there was that moment in time, ten years ago. For thirty years Twin had been in the practice of conducting a children's Christmas pageant in the parish church before the first Mass on Christmas Eve. Each year the pageant was written by Twin and followed a different theme. Since Pope Benedict had declared this to be a year honoring St. Paul, the pageant was dedicated to that saint. All of the readings were excerpts from the writings of St. Paul. The pageant began with the instrumental playing of an Easter hymn and the words, "All I want is to know Christ Jesus and the power flowing from his Resurrection…" On that particular evening, just as Twin was about to go up to the microphone and welcome the congregation, she recognized the faces of four people walking into church – her sister, brother-in-law, and a niece and nephew. What a total surprise! The pageant went on without a flaw. The thirty-five children fulfilled their roles perfectly. They processed from the sanctuary at the end wearing white stoles and carrying candles, symbols of their being born anew in Baptism, one of the main themes in the letters of St. Paul. This was the most colorful, the most creative pageant that Twin had ever directed – the very best ever.

Responding: Listeners take turns contributing their responses to the story | Up to 4 minutes

We then offered the storyteller what we noticed, appreciated, and wondered about as she told her story. We offered our comments not to demonstrate that we had connected and found the essence of her story; **we offered our observations in an effort to help her connect with and find more of the essence in her own story.** The three of us who listened took turns relaying what we had noticed in her story, what we had appreciated, what we had wondered about.

- I noticed your immense love for your family, for God, for your vocation.
- I appreciated your fidelity to your vocation, and your willingness to speak about the difficulties and challenges you've experienced in religious life. I haven't had the privilege of hearing other religious women speak about that aspect of their lives.

- I wondered what it felt like to tell us this story today. What did you notice in your story as you shared it with us?
- I noticed how enlivened your voice became as you spoke about writing and producing the Christmas pageants.
- I too noticed your enthusiasm about these creative endeavors. I wondered what kinds of creative projects you are currently working on and enjoying.
- I appreciated the part of the story where you described purposely passing by your family as they walked up the front sidewalk, opening the door of the convent, and stepping inside ahead of your sister. I noticed how your voice really perked up when you mentioned that unprecedented behavior. Instead of following, Twin led.
- I too appreciated Twin's chutzpah, and her willingness to claim what was deep in her own heart. It reminded me to keep doing the same.
- It led me to wonder, what is stirring deep in your heart at this time in your life that you would like to claim?

And on it went. For up to four minutes, we took turns noticing, appreciating, and wondering together about what more was waiting to be revealed in Twin's story.

Retelling: The speaker describes what s/he is discovering about her or his story | Up to 4 minutes

Sister Elise then had up to four minutes to respond to our noticings, appreciatings, and wonderings. Most of that time she devoted to talking about the enjoyment she derives from her creative work. She told us more about how she had written the scripts for the Christmas pageants, and how she had never repeated the same script twice. Instead, she had challenged herself to create something new for each year's pageant. She spoke of how much she loved working with the students and their families, and the joy it brought to see the students play their parts in these productions. She talked about how she would love to do more creative work at this time in her life, and is discerning what form that might take. She spoke of the current relationship she and her sister now share, her gratitude for her vocation, her love of God, and her family.

And after she spoke, she paused, grinned, and then remarked, "I can't believe how I could learn so much in fifteen minutes."

Pausing: In silence and gratitude, we honored what she had shared | Up to 1 minute

***

A couple of weeks later, I received the following email from Sister Elise:

Diane,

It's hard to believe it's already three weeks since the workshop at St. Catherine University. What an awesome experience that was! I did learn some things that were helpful to me as a spiritual director, but even more, I did the processing of my own story, which I really needed to do. Thank you so much! Those days were very valuable to me personally. And the story continues. I really got into writing, and I want to keep doing it.

When we wrote our protagonist stories, I wrote about being a twin. You came to my small group for the sharing of our stories. You invited me to finish the story and said you would be interested in seeing it. Well, I finished it today. I was surprised at the turn it took. It ended up being a story about re-creation.

I'm passing the story on to you, for whatever it's worth. If you find it helpful and want to include it in some of your writing, that's fine with me. You may also attach my name, if you so choose.

Enjoy these beautiful autumn days. May you and your family have a blessed Thanksgiving.

Sister Elise Cholewinski, OSF

***

Her attached story retold the story she had shared with us at the workshop. Yet, this version of the story now featured a new ending:

Christmas dinner was different that year. There was a different topic of conversation. As Twin sat at the table, she no longer felt stuck in a corner. She was no long half a person, trudging through life in another's shadow. Her unique gifts had been on display; she was being recognized and applauded. She was being validated for who she is. Twin's face beamed more brightly than the biggest Christmas star. She was home; she was whole. That Christmas was truly an Easter event, the first day of a New Creation. Those words from St. Paul were being fulfilled in Twin's own being. She knew Christ Jesus to be alive in her; she felt the power of his Resurrection flowing in the depths of her own person. Winter had turned into spring.

As Sister Elise observed in her email to me: *And the story continues. . . .*

Each of our stories continues. I hope that you will invite one or more participants to gather to begin, or continue, exploring your story.

May you, like she, be surprised at the turns your story takes.

And may your stories, like hers, end up being stories of re-creation.

Conclusion

Who knows how I might have turned out if my father had lived, but through the loss of him all those years ago I think that I learned something about how even tragedy can be a means of grace that I might never come to any other way. As I see it, in other words, God acts in history and in your and my brief histories not as the puppeteer who sets the scene and works the strings but rather as the great director who no matter what role fate casts us in conveys to us somehow from the wings, if we have our eyes, ears, hearts open and sometimes even if we don't, how we can play those roles in a way to enrich and ennoble and hallow the whole vast drama of things including our own small but crucial parts in it.

—Frederick Buechner,
Telling Secrets

It has been over eighty years since Frederick Buechner's father committed suicide. Buechner was ten at the time. Since then, the question *who knows how I might have turned out if my father had lived* has infused the over thirty books of fiction and non-fiction he has written. He acknowledges that he will never be finished telling this story.

And we will never be finished telling ours.

Kim Stafford reflects on the story of his brother's suicide in his book, *100 Tricks Every Boy Can Do: How My Brother Disappeared,*

165

"...the whole story had seemed impossible to tell, too big and too strange. This story had been a silence in my family for twenty-four years. Only by telling it in little sips, some half a page, some half a dozen pages, could I bring it forth at last."[xxxvii]

Stafford underscores, "The more mysterious dimensions of the story were the ones I most needed to tell, or try to tell." And he found, "I wrestled with how to tell it at every stage."

I know this is true for me, and I suspect it is for you: it's the more mysterious dimensions of our lives that we most need to tell, or try to tell. And indeed, we too will wrestle with how to do so.

That is why, as psychologist Dan McAdams reminds us, *telling our story* is as much a redemptive act as the acts that are told.

In *The Suicide Index*, Joan Wickersham wrestled with how to tell the story of what it was like to lose a family member to suicide. She took the experience of her father's suicide apart and attempted to put it back together through an index of themes: "I'm writing because I need to understand the story of my family. But I'm also appropriating it, trying to transform it into something I can understand."[xxxviii]

While there are no guarantees that *through their telling our stories will be transformed into something that we can understand,* I do believe that **we will be transformed through their telling.**

Recently, my spiritual director Lois asked me about the impact that writing this book has had on me. The answer can be found in the book's title. The reason I named this book, *Re-Creating a Life,* is because I have felt that through its writing, my life has been re-created.

Telling these stories to you the reader required me to continue asking myself:

What is the truest, most authentic story I can tell *at this moment in time* about this lived experience?

Moreover, writing this book has helped me to see *how I have been re-created* through the life I have actually lived, rather than the one I had imagined I would.

I am intrigued by how I no longer feel the pain of the phantom life I wrote about in the prologue. In its place, I have noticed an increasing sense of gratitude, courage, and compassion arising in me.

I'm eager to see how much more generative my life may become now that I have learned how to tell a more redemptive story about it.

However, I also remind myself that I am not yet finished telling my story, nor will I ever be. My story, like yours, continues to evolve. Even though my story of re-creation is now in print, it is not set in stone. Creation continues.

The sad things that happened long ago will always remain part of who we are just as the glad and gracious things will too, but instead of being a burden of guilt, recrimination, and regret that makes us constantly stumble as we go, even the saddest things can become, once we have made peace with them, a source of wisdom and strength for the journey that lies ahead. It is through memory that we are able to reclaim much of our lives that we have long since written off by finding that in everything that has happened to us over the years God was offering up possibilities of new life and healing which, though we may have missed them at the time, we can still choose and be brought to life by and healed by all these years later. Another way of saying it, perhaps, is that memory makes it possible for us both to bless the past, even those parts of it that we have always felt cursed by, and also to be blessed by it.

—Frederick Buechner,
Telling Secrets

I pray that I may continue to glean more interpretations and perspectives on the stories I have shared here with you, and I look forward to reading and hearing about what you have discovered through the telling of your own.

***

Appendices

Appendix One:
Conversation Covenant

Regardless of whether your group meets for only one or many storytelling sessions, inviting everyone to practice and uphold the following agreements increases safety and trust among those gathered.

Before you begin, take turns reading the following agreements aloud.

Listen Well…

- I will listen to others in a compassionate and nonjudgmental way. I aspire to *listen within*, with the ear of my heart, as I listen to others speak;
- I will encourage and honor my own and others' questions. It is not my responsibility to analyze, fix, save, or advise others in the group;
- I will offer the gift of presence by turning off any devices that may distract others or me.

Speak Truth…

- I will speak the truth of my heart as I offer the insights, joys, struggles, and questions that are a part of my journey;
- I will speak for myself, in the first person, as I relay my experiences, feelings, perceptions, attitudes, and beliefs (e.g., "I wonder about …" or "I felt…");
- I will speak directly to a group participant if clarification about something s/he said is needed;

- I will feel free to remain silent and tell the group if I would like to pass.

Be Attentive…

- I will observe time limits. I will limit my storytelling and responding to the time allotted;
- I will refrain from side conversations or references to conversations with others in the group who I know well;
- I will maintain "double confidentiality." What is shared in the group stays in the group. Moreover, I will not approach any of our group's participants with feedback outside of our meeting time unless it is asked for.

After you have finished, check in to see what, if any, clarifications are needed about one or more of the agreements. Ask participants if there are any more agreements they would like to add. Some communities may find it helpful to sign the agreements in the presence of one another.

It often proves helpful to return to the agreements at subsequent sessions in an effort to hold oneself and one another accountable to this way practicing presence in your conversation.

For more information regarding the logistics of convening and facilitating such a storytelling group, please see my first book, *Conversation—The Sacred Art.*

Appendix Two:
The 4, 4, 4 Storytelling Format

Telling: The focus person shares their story in response to one of the story telling prompts featured in the chapters of this book | **Up to 4 minutes**

Responding: Listeners take turns contributing their responses to the story | **Up to 4 minutes**

- I noticed. . .

- I appreciated . . .

- I wondered. . .

Retelling: The focus person describes what s/he is discovering about her or his story | **Up to 4 minutes**

Pausing: Participants share time in silence to honor what has been shared | **Up to 1 minute**

Appendix Three:
The 4 R's of Deep Listening

To "listen" another's soul into a condition of disclosure and discovery may be almost the greatest service that any human being ever performs for another.

—Douglas Steere,
Gleanings: A Random Harvest

---

1. **Respect the sacredness within us, between us, and beyond us**. We pause in silence at the beginning, end, and throughout our conversation to increase our awareness of the sacred.

2. **Refrain from offering interpretations**. As we listen to others' stories, our role is not to interpret the meaning of how Mystery is at work in their lives. Rather, our role is to encourage them *to ferret it out for themselves*, as Frederick Buechner observes:

   ". . . life itself can be thought of as an alphabet by which God graciously makes known his presence and purpose and power among us. Like the Hebrew alphabet, the alphabet of grace has no vowels, and in that sense his words to us are always veiled, subtle, cryptic, so that it is left to us to delve their meaning, to fill in the vowels, for ourselves by means of all the faith and imagination we can muster. God speaks to us in such a way, presumably, not because he chooses to be obscure but because, unlike a dictionary word whose meaning is fixed, the meaning of an incarnate word is the meaning it has for the one it is spoken to, the meaning that becomes clear and effective in our lives only when we ferret it out for ourselves."[xxxix]

3. **Remain curious and adopt *a not-knowing position*.** We trust that there is something we can learn from each and every story we hear. Therefore, we intentionally set aside what we think we know about one another's stories as well as bracket whatever expertise we bring. We limit our response to what we noticed, appreciated and wondered about as we listened, in an effort to help storytellers *generate their own interpretations* of their narrative.

4. **Remind one another that our stories are never complete or finished.** We invite one another to hold our stories lightly not tightly, as we continue mining the meaning in our narratives. We recognize that any story that we tell is both just a story and there is more to the story; any story we tell is ultimately incomplete.

Notes

[i] Alice Morgan, *What is Narrative Therapy? An Easy-to-Read Introduction* (Adelaide, South Australia: Dulwich Centre Publications, 2000), 8.

[ii] Narrative therapists invite clients to develop their own names for their stories. The story's name is then capitalized to both honor and underscore that we *stand in relationship to* our stories.

[iii] Psychologists report that the majority of adults remain in a socialized mindset, failing to develop the capacity for self-authorship. See Robert Kegan and Lisa Laskow Lahey's, *Immunity to Change: How to Overcome It and Unlock the Potential In Yourself and Your Organization* (Boston, MA: Harvard Business Publishing Corporation, 2009).

[iv] A community of concern is "a group of people whom an individual or community has chosen to come alongside them in their journey of living into an **alternative story** for their lives." See Chené Swart, *Re-Authoring the World The Narrative Lens and Practices for Organisations, Communities and Individuals* (Randburg, South Africa: Knowres Publishing, 2013), 167.

[v] Ibid, 15.

[vi] Swart subsequently named the business she founded: Transformations. For more information visit: www.transformations.co.za.

[vii] *Lives Explored* is a production of the Collegeville Institute Seminars on Vocation and is funded through the generosity of the Lilly Endowment, Inc. Visit www.lives-explored.com to view Francois's story and the entire collection of narratives featured in this series.

[viii] Dan P. McAdams is a professor of psychology and human development at Northwestern University. He and his research team have found that highly generative adults tell their life stories with an emphasis on the theme of personal redemption. See his book, *The Redemptive Self: Stories Americans Live By*, rev. ed. (New York: Oxford University Press, 2013).

[ix] David Drake, *Narrative Coaching: The Definitive Guide to Bringing Stories to Life*, 2nd ed. (Petaluma, CA: CNC Press, 2018), 303.

[x] John S. Dunne, *The Way of All the Earth: Experiments in Truth and Religion* (Notre Dame, IN: Notre Dame University Press, 1978).

[xi] Mary Catherine Bateson, *Composing a Life* (New York: Grove Press, 1989), 16.

[xii] HyoJu Lee, *Redeeming Singleness: Postmodern Pastoral Care and Counseling for Never-Married Single Women* (Eugene, OR: Wipf & Stock, 2017). HyoJu Lee sought to better understand the experience of never-married, Protestant Korean-American women under 30 who, like herself, feel marginalized. Through her interviews, she invited them to give voice to their own truths of being single in a culture that so valued marriage. She explored the stories they told themselves as

they contended with the sociocultural script dominant in their Korean culture asserting that *your life doesn't really begin until you are married.*

[xiii] Michael White, one of the founders of narrative therapy, invites readers to "take a new look at their own lives and find a new significance in events often neglected, to find sparkling actions that are often discounted, to find fascination in experiences previously overlooked; and to find solutions to problems and predicaments in landscapes often previously considered bereft." Quoted in David Denborough, *Retelling the Stories of Our Lives: Everyday Narrative Therapy to Draw Inspiration and Transform Experience* (New York: W.W. Norton & Company, 2014), x.

[xiv] Denborough, *Retelling the Stories of Our Lives*, 25-57.

[xv] Adler acknowledged that our recollections might vary from the actual facts of what happened. Nonetheless, his interest was on how people *constructed* these earliest recollections. Heinz L. Ansbacher, "Adler's Interpretation of Early Recollections: Historical Account" accessed February 6, 2019.
https://pdfs.semanticscholar.org/5355/208088e78b6618f341a12093781ed21e06b9.pdf

[xvi] Ray Bradbury, *Zen in the Art of Writing* (Santa Barbara, CA: Joshua Odell Editions, 1996), 21.

[xvii] Michael White writes about the importance of Re-Membering Conversations. White describes how each of our identities is shaped by "significant figures and identities of a person's past, present and projected future." Re-Membering conversations invite us to consider

a figure's contribution to our identity, and may include a consideration of our contribution to theirs. White emphasizes: "There are many options with regard to the identification of figures and identities that might be remembered in people's lives. These figures and identities do not have to be directly known in order to be significant in re-membering conversations. For example, they may be the authors of books that have been important or characters from movies or comics. Nor do these figures and identities have to be people; they could be the stuffed toys of a person's childhood or a favorite pet. See Michael White, *Maps of Narrative Practice* (New York: Norton, 2007), 129.

[xviii] Chino Otsuka, *Imagine Finding Me: Images and Words by Chino Otsuka* (United Kingdom, Trace Editions, 2006).

[xix] The Naikan approach was developed by Yoshimoto Ishin, a Japanese Shin Buddhist. See Gregg Krech, *Question Your Life: Naikan Self-Reflection and the Transformation of Our Stories* (Monkton, VT: ToDo Institute Books, 2017), 83-4.

[xx] Dave Isay, *Ties That Bind: Stories of Love and Gratitude from the First Ten Years of StoryCorps* (New York: Penguin Press, 2013), 2–3.

[xxi] StoryCorps.org features numerous examples of questions one can ask along with a wide assortment of past interviews that have been conducted.

[xxii] See Howard Thurman's "The Sound of the Genuine," Baccalaureate Address at Spelman College, May 4, 1980, edited by Jo

Moore Stewart for The Spelman Messenger 96 no. 4 (Summer 1980): 14–15.

[xxiii] This retreat activity is inspired by the work of photographer Jim Brandenburg. In 1994, Brandenburg vowed that the shutter of his camera would open and close **only once** each day for ninety days. His self-imposed project is featured in the documentary, *Chased by the Light*, as well as a book by the same name. See Jim Brandenburg's *Chased by the Light*, 2nd ed. (Minneapolis, MN: Creative Publishing International, 2001).

[xxiv] Christine Valters Paintner observes in *Eyes of the Heart: Photography as a Christian Contemplative Practice:* "'Taking' photos with the head is often an act of analysis or grasping, as when we try to either capture an image or make one that is aesthetically pleasing. 'Receiving' photos with the heart is an experience of grace and revelation, an encounter with the sacred" (Notre Dame, IN: Sorin Books, 2013), 19.

[xxv] A paten is a small plate used to hold Eucharistic bread, which is to be consecrated during the Mass.

[xxvi] Howard Thurman, *The Mood of Christmas* (Richmond, IN: Friends United Press, 1973), 24.

[xxvii] Ira Progroff, *At a Journal Workshop: Writing to Access the Power of the Unconscious and Evoke Creative Ability* (New York: G. P. Putnam's Sons, 1975).

[xxviii] http://publishedwritingsofmaxreif.jimdo.com

[xxix] Arthur Green, *Ehyeh: A Kabbalah for Tomorrow* (Woodstock, VT: Jewish Lights Publishing, 2003), 104.

[xxx] Quote attributed to Metropolitan Anthony of Sourozh, source unknown.

[xxxi] Pagan Kennedy, "How to Cultivate the Art of Serendipity," *New York Times,* January 2, 2016, accessed February 6, 2019. www.nytimes.com/2016/01/03/opinion/how-to-cultivate-the-art-of-serendipity.html.

[xxxii] Legend has it that Ernest Hemingway was once challenged to write a story in only six words. His response? "For sale: baby shoes, never worn." In November 2006, Larry Smith, founder of SMITH Magazine, gave the six-word novel a personal twist by asking his community to describe their lives in exactly six words. The Six-Word Memoir project was born. See www.sixwordmemoirs.com, accessed on December 18, 2018. Also see *Not Quite What I Was Planning: Six-Word Memoirs by Writers Famous and Obscure*, eds. Rachel Fershleiser and Larry Smith (New York: Harper Collins Publishers, 2008).

[xxxiii] Nelle Morton, *The Journey Is Home* (Boston, MA: Beacon Press, 1985), 204-5.

[xxxiv] Stipulating and upholding time limits, that is, ensuring that each participant has the same amount of time to both tell their story and receive others' observations about their story, engenders trust and safety in groups. A recent study of over a hundred small groups at Google confirmed the benefits of "equality in distribution of conversational turn-taking." Researchers observed that in the most

effective groups, team members spoke in roughly the same proportion. On some teams, everyone spoke during each task; on others, leadership shifted among teammates from assignment to assignment. But in each case, by the end of the day, everyone had spoken roughly the same amount. Charles Duhigg, "What Google Learned From Its Quest to Build the Perfect Team," *New York Times,* Feb 25, 2016, accessed February 6, 2019.

http://www.nytimes.com/2016/02/28/magazine/what-google-learned-from-its-quest-to-build-the-perfect-team.html

[xxxv] James Pennebaker's finding regarding fifteen minutes of writing time has been confirmed in the workshops I have led. Participants report that fifteen minutes provides enough spaciousness, yet not so much that one begins editing, overthinking, or rehearsing what one intends to say. To learn more, see: James Pennebaker and Joshua Smyth, *Opening Up by Writing It Down: How Expressive Writing Improves Health and Eases Emotional Pain,* 3rd ed. (New York: The Guilford Press, 2016).

[xxxvi] Robert Sardello, *Silence: The Mystery of Wholeness* (Berkeley, CA: North Atlantic Books, 2006), 49.

[xxxvii] Kim Stafford, "100 Tricks Every Boy Can Do: How My Brother Disappeared," chap. 18 in *Writing Hard Stories: Celebrated Memoirists Who Shaped Art from Trauma* (Boston, MA: Beacon Press, 2017), 202.

[xxxviii] Joan Wickersham, *The Suicide Index: Putting My Father's Death in Order* (New York: Mariner Books, 2008), 185.

[xxxix] Frederick Buechner, *The Sacred Journey* (New York: HarperCollins Publishers, 1982), 4.

For Further Learning

Baldwin, Christina. *Storycatcher: Making Sense of Our Lives through the Power and Practice of Story.* Novato, CA: New World Library, 2005.

Brooks, Melanie. *Writing Hard Stories: Celebrated Memoirists Who Shaped Art from Trauma.* Boston, MA: Beacon Press, 2017.

Buechner, Frederick. *The Remarkable Ordinary: How to Stop, Look, and Listen to Life.* Grand Rapids, MI: Zondervan, 2017.

Buechner, Frederick. *Telling Secrets.* New York: HarperCollins Publishers, 1991.

Cahalan, Kathleen A. *The Stories We Live: Finding God's Calling All Around Us.* Grand Rapids, MI: Wm. B. Eerdmans Publishing Co., 2017.

Coyle, Suzanne M. *Uncovering Spiritual Narratives: Using Story in Pastoral Care and Ministry.* Minneapolis, MN: Fortress Press, 2014.

Denborough, David. *Retelling the Stories of Our Lives: Everyday Narrative Therapy to Draw Inspiration and Transform Experience.* New York: W.W. Norton & Company, 2014.

DeSalvo, Louise. *Writing as a Way of Healing: How Telling Our Stories Transforms Our Lives.* New York: HarperCollins Publishers, 1999.

Drake, David B. *Narrative Coaching: The Definitive Guide to Bringing Stories to Life* (2nd ed.). Petaluma, CA: CNC Press, 2018.

Hester, Richard L., and Kelli Walker-Jones. *Know Your Story and Lead with It: The Power of Narrative in Clergy Leadership.* Herndon, VA: Alban Institute, 2009.

Kotre, John. *Make It Count: How to Generate a Legacy that Gives Meaning to Your Life.* New York: The Free Press, 1999.

Krech, Gregg. *Question Your Life: Naikan Self-Reflection and the Transformation of Our Stories.* Monkton, VT: ToDo Institute Books, 2017.

Magolda, Marcia Baxter. *Authoring Your Life: Developing an Internal Voice to Navigate Life's Challenges.* Sterling, VA: Stylus Publishing, LLC, 2009.

Marinella, Sandra. *The Story You Need to Tell: Writing to Heal from Trauma, Illness or Loss.* Novato, CA: New World Library, 2017.

McAdams, Dan P. *The Art and Science of Personality Development.* New York: Guilford Press, 2015.

McAdams, Dan P. *The Redemptive Self: Stories Americans Live By* (rev. ed.). New York: Oxford University Press, 2013.

McAdams, Dan P. *The Stories We Live By: Personal Myths and the Making of the Self.* New York: William Morrow, 1993.

Millis, Diane M., and Busshō Lahn. "Narrative Stances in Spiritual Direction: Hearing Others to Their Life-Giving Story." *Presence:*

An International Journal of Spiritual Direction 24, no. 4 (2018): 5-12.

Millis, Diane M. "Opening the Lens of the Heart: Looking Out at the World, Seeing Inside Ourselves." *Presence: An International Journal of Spiritual Direction* 23, no. 3 (2017): 22-28.

Millis, Diane M. *Deepening Engagement: Essential Wisdom for Listening and Leading with Purpose, Meaning and Joy.* Woodstock, VT: SkyLight Paths Publishing, 2015.

Millis, Diane M. *Conversation—the Sacred Art: Practicing Presence in an Age of Distraction.* Woodstock, VT: SkyLight Paths Publishing, 2013.

Millis, Diane M. "Cultivating Compassion through Group Spiritual Companioning." *Presence: An International Journal of Spiritual Direction* 18, no. 3 (2012): 6–14.

Morgan, Alice. *What is Narrative Therapy? An Easy-to-Read Introduction.* Adelaide, South Australia: Dulwich Centre Publications, 2000.

Morton, Nelle. *The Journey Is Home.* Boston, MA: Beacon Press, 1985.

Ochs, Carol. *Our Lives as Torah: Finding God in Our Own Stories.* San Francisco, CA: Jossey-Bass, 2001.

Pennebaker, James, and Joshua Smyth. *Opening Up by Writing It Down: How Expressive Writing Improves Health and Eases Emotional Pain,* 3rd ed. (New York: The Guilford Press, 2016).

Ruffing, Janet K. *To Tell the Sacred Tale: Spiritual Direction and Narrative.* New York: Paulist Press, 2011.

Swart, Chené. *Re-Authoring the World: The Narrative Lens and Practices for Organisations, Communities and Individuals.* Randburg, South Africa: Knowres Publishing, 2013.

White, Michael. *Maps of Narrative Practice.* New York: Norton, 2007.

Wimberly, Edward. *Recalling Our Own Stories: Spiritual Renewal for Religious Caregivers.* San Francisco, CA: Jossey-Bass Inc, 1997.

Acknowledgments

We need a community in order to learn how to tell our most life-giving story, and I am grateful for the life-giving community of conversation partners who accompanied me as I wrote this book.

Thank you Kristen Hobby for being on board from the beginning, for reading various iterations of the entire manuscript, and devoting numerous hours to Skype conversations with me.

Thank you Kami Pohl for your engaging participation in recent workshops I offered, and for your gracious willingness to read the entire book to help me ensure alignment between the workshop and written versions of this approach.

Thank you Kyle Homstad for offering such constructive feedback at the onset of this project as I formulated the table of contents and initial chapters, and for generously contributed a story of your own to it.

Thank you Jennifer Jinks Hoffmann, Vic Klimoski, Busshō Lahn, Barbara Redmond, and Jeannie Roberts for responding to portions of the manuscript at key moments in the writing process.

Thank you Vicki Richardson, Natalie Thoresen, and Sister Elise Cholewinski, OSF, for entrusting me with your stories and giving me permission to feature them in this book.

From the time I was a child, I have been fascinated with hearing into speech others' stories. As an adult, I have been blessed with numerous colleagues who have helped me to hone my skills and develop the approach I've written about in this book.

Thank you Patrick Henry for introducing me to the first person method, the Collegeville approach, for articulating our theologies in the context of our life stories. I had the pleasure of practicing this approach during my time at the Collegeville Institute initially as a resident scholar and later as a summer consultation participant. It was Patrick who first called my attention to the work of Frederick Buechner, and encouraged me to turn my focus from writing for other professors to writing for the public.

Thank you to my colleagues at the Lilly Endowment, Inc., for funding our initiative, *Companions on a Journey*. This grant enabled those of us at the College of Saint Benedict to form, train, and equip our undergraduate students in the process of group spiritual accompaniment. Thank you Sister Mary Reuter, OSB, and Christine Luna Munger for the wisdom and passion you brought to our collaboration, and to all those in our community who contributed and participated.

Thank you Rev. Amy Zalk Larson for inviting me to bring the *Journey Conversations* approach, for connecting story-to-story, to your ministry at Luther College. I learned so much from our work together with Sheila Radford-Hill, Sandhya Purohit Caton, and the many students, faculty, and staff members who participated. It was Sandhya who first introduced me to thinking of our stories as prisms.

Thank you Kathleen Cahalan and Laura Kelly Fanucci at the Collegeville Institute for investing in and helping me to implement the vision I had for creating an educational narrative video series, *Lives Explored*, depicting how we discern our life's callings and purpose.

Thank you Sharon Tan, at United Theological Seminary of the Twin Cites, for inviting me to serve as a consultant for the grant you received from the Association of Theological Schools whose primary aim was to teach our seminary students how to tell redemptive stories. The grant's theory of change was based upon the research findings of psychologist Dan McAdams, and his team at Northwestern University's Foley Center for the Study of Lives, that those who tell stories featuring more redemptive sequences tend to lead more generative lives. As the author of the grant, Sharon believed it was essential that our students, these future ministry leaders, as well as the faculty who teach them increase their awareness of their narrative identity. Towards that end, I was charged with leading workshops for the seminary faculty as well as designing a new course on narrative approaches to spiritual formation for the students. Thank you to the students who accompanied me in the course, *How Our Stories Shape Our Leadership*, as well as the faculty, administration, and staff at United for their engagement with this project.

It has been an honor and a pleasure to work with the leadership team at Spiritual Director's International as they launch their newly minted publishing press.

Thank you Rev. Seifu Anil Singh-Molares, Executive Director at SDI, for the gift of your enthusiasm and continual encouragement of this project, Steven Crandell, Director of Content, for your editorial guidance and remarkable capacity for honoring my agency as an author, Rory Briski, Chief Operating Officer, for contributing your publishing expertise and guidance every step of the way, Matt

189

Whitney, Visual Media and Technology Coordinator, for creating such a beautiful vision for the design of the book, and Maud Naveau, Events and Journeys Manager, for your hospitable assistance with coordinating workshops and seminars based upon this book.

I continue to learn more about how to tell a life-giving story through monthly gatherings with my spiritual director and spirituality group. Thank you Lois Lindbloom, Mary Cavanaugh, Chris McPartland, Jim Diedrich Smith, and Lew Zeidner for the stories and friendship we have shared over the course of the past decade.

Closer to home, thank you Rosemary Cooper, my mother and my exemplar. Over the course of your life, I have witnessed how you have consistently chosen to tell a redemptive story. I can only hope to be as courageous and resilient as you are, and to live my life as generatively as you have lived yours.

I know that I would not be telling the story I am currently telling were it not for my husband Mark Millis. He is one of the finest listeners with whom I have ever had the pleasure of conversing. Thank you Mark for your kindness and tender care for me. Sharing life with you has healed my heart and restored my spirit in ways I may never be able to fully convey.

My other treasured listener is our son Ryan to whom this book is dedicated. Thank you Ryan for the immense joy you bring to our lives, and for inspiring us to tell a more life-giving story through the manner in which you tell your own.

Credits

Grateful acknowledgment is given for permission to use the following:

Max Reif, "To a Visionary Whose Name I'll Never Know," © Max Reif, Used by permission.

About the Author

Diane M. Millis, PhD, loves to help people explore their own stories as a way to discover meaning, purpose, and joy in their lives.

She is a spiritual director and the author of *Conversation—The Sacred Art: Practicing Presence in an Age of Distraction* (SkyLight Paths Publishing, 2013) and *Deepening Engagement: Essential Wisdom for Listening and Leading with Purpose, Meaning and Joy* (SkyLight Paths Publishing, 2015).

Diane has taught at the University of Minnesota, the College of Saint Benedict/Saint John's University, and Saint Catherine University. She currently teaches at United Theological Seminary of the Twin Cities.

She is the founder of *Companions on a Journey* at the College of Saint Benedict, funded by the Lilly Endowment, Inc., and the *Journey Conversations Project*. She served as host and producer of *Lives Explored* for the Collegeville Institute. Diane has also served as a coach and consultant for the Lilly Endowment, Inc., working with leadership teams at colleges, universities, and theological schools throughout the United States.

Diane shares her life with her husband Mark and their young adult son Ryan. She and Mark live in Minneapolis.

In addition to teaching, program development, and writing, she is a popular conference presenter and retreat facilitator for participants in a wide array of sectors—educational, non-profit, philanthropic, health care, and corporate.

To learn more: www.dianemillis.com.

Diane M. Millis, PhD

Author Photo by: Bruce Challgren

Made in the USA
Middletown, DE
04 May 2019